STORIES
for the
CHRISTIAN YEAR

STORIES
for the
CHRISTIAN
YEAR

The Chrysostom Society

Edited by Eugene H. Peterson

COLLIER BOOKS
Macmillan Publishing Company *New York*
Maxwell Macmillan Canada *Toronto*
Maxwell Macmillan International
New York Oxford Singapore Sydney

Collier Books	Maxwell Macmillan Canada, Inc.
Macmillan Publishing Company	1200 Eglinton Avenue East
866 Third Avenue	Suite 200
New York, NY 10022	Don Mills, Ontario M3C 3N1

Macmillan Publishing Company is part of the Maxwell Communication Group of Companies.

The following essays first appeared in *Christianity Today:* "Christmas," © 1989 by Eugene H. Peterson; "Maundy Thursday," © 1989 by Walter Wangerin, Jr.; "Good Friday," © 1989 by Virginia Stem Owens; "Holy Saturday," © 1989 by Eugene H. Peterson; "Easter Sunday," © 1989 by Philip Yancey.

The following essay first appeared in *Modern Liturgy:* "Solemnity of Mary," © 1991 by Emilie Griffin.

Excerpt from "A Shropshire Lad"—Authorised Edition—from *The Collected Poems of A. E. Housman.* Copyright 1939, 1940, © 1965 by Holt, Rhinehart and Winston. Copyright © 1967, 1968 by Robert E. Symons. Reprinted by permission of Henry Holt and Company, Inc.

Excerpt from "Ash-Wednesday" in *Collected Poems 1909–1962,* copyright 1936 by Harcourt Brace Jovanovich, Inc., copyright © 1964, 1963 by T. S. Eliot, reprinted by permission of the publisher.

Excerpts from "The Day With a White Mark" from *Poems* by C. S. Lewis, edited by Walter Hooper, copyright © 1964 by the Executors of the Estate of C. S. Lewis, reprinted by permission of Harcourt Brace Jovanovich, Inc.

Library of Congress Cataloging-in-Publication Data
Stories for the Christian year / the Chrysostom Society; edited
  by Eugene H. Peterson. — 1st Collier Books ed.
      p. cm.
    ISBN 0-02-028185-4
    1. Christian fiction, American. I. Peterson, Eugene H., date.
    II. Chrysostom Society. III. Title: Stories for the Christian year.
  [PS648.C43S75   1994]   93-6526   CIP
  813'.0108382—dc20

Macmillan books are available at special discounts for bulk purchases for sales promotions, premiums, fund-raising, or educational use. For details, contact:

Special Sales Director
Macmillan Publishing Company
866 Third Avenue
New York, NY 10022

First Collier Books Edition 1994

10 9 8 7 6 5 4 3 2 1

Printed in the United States of America

CONTENTS

Contents

INTRODUCTION

We keep time by observing the sun and the moon; we keep sane by telling stories. Telling time and stories have a happy conjunction in what is often referred to as "the Christian year."

A calendar without a story is inadequate. It is hardly worth arriving at a place on the right day if we don't know who we are when we get there, if we don't know what to do. Stories tell us who we are, tell us what we can do. It was an extraordinary achievement of the ancient mind to mark off accurately months, weeks, and days in our annual trip around the sun. The achievement was of considerable moment in agriculture, commerce, and government. But these planetary calculations, useful as they are, do not suffice. They tell us that time is; they don't tell us what time is for. So the days and months acquired names with accompanying stories, not just numbers. Arithmetic was subordinated to narrative.

Christians inherited a Roman calendar that was perfectly adequate for getting up in the morning and going to bed on time, for calculating the equinox, for setting a wedding day. But the Roman stories attached to the Roman calendar were not at all adequate. So from early days Christians told stories of Jesus and their experience with him. As the stories were told and retold, they clustered around the calendar and pushed the Roman stories off; they were better stories. In a few years the calendar, even while all the numbers stayed the same, was transformed in shape and meaning. The "Roman" year slowly gave way to a "Christian" year.

The Christian year is divided into two parts, roughly equal—our Lord's half-year and the Christian's half-year. Our Lord's half-year, from Advent to Ascension, tells the stories of our Lord's arrival, life, death, and resurrection. The Christian's half-year (from Pentecost to Christ the King) tells the stories of our reception of his Spirit, our participation in the Trinity, our long discipleship as a communion of saints, our death and resurrection under the overarching sovereignty of Christ.

The stories that we tell of our Lord provoke stories that we tell of ourselves as men and women who experience our Lord. For every Christ story there is a Christian story, for Christ lives and continues to live in us, and the life comes out in story form.

But not everyone these days sees the calendar as storybook, let alone a Christian storybook. The calendar is being subjected to widespread secularization. With the erosion of stories, calendars characteristically show up attached to nudes, great and not-so-great art, cartoons, photographs of the wilderness, family pets, and quotations in calligraphy. The large and easy interior rhythms of a year that moves from birth, life, death, resurrection on to spirit, obedience, faith, and blessing have been lost in the jerky, ill-timed, and insensitive interruptions by public-relations campaigns, school openings and closings, sales days, tax deadlines, inventories, and elections. Advent is buried under "shopping days before Christmas." The joyful disciplines of Lent are exchanged for the anxious pentitentials of filling out income tax forms.

So as the forces of greed and lust and ambition move in on the calendar, trying to force the Christian stories off and recoup the honored place they had before the Christians made their move 2,000 years ago, my friends and I thought it timely to tell Christian year stories again: tell the stories of our year, the stories that define and shape our beginnings and ends, our living and dying, our rebirths and blessings—and behind and in it all, the story of our God revealed in our Lord Jesus Christ.

—*Eugene H. Peterson*

STORIES
for the
CHRISTIAN YEAR

ADVENT

➤➥

Alice Slaikeu Lawhead

On the first Sunday in December, I sit in church and hear these words:

> *Now is the time to wake out of sleep: for now our salvation*
> *is nearer than when we first believed.*

And I think: now is the time to make a purposeful trip to the supermarket and do the shopping for all the baking that needs to be done. Now is the time to make sure all the church programs and neighborhood parties and school activities are penciled in on the calendar so we don't overbook like we did last year. And if we really are going to get a goose for Christmas dinner, then now is the time to order it from the butcher.

Now is the time to pick up last year's party dress from the cleaners! Now is the time to get up in the attic and dig out the Christmas decorations! Now is the time to get the children to the barber, and see if we can't get the carpets shampooed before the open house on the fourteenth, and call the university to see if they have any decent tickets left for this year's performance of *A Christmas Carol*.

Mrs. Williams has stepped to the lectern for the New Testament reading. I hear her proclaiming something about dates and times, my friends, and how we know perfectly well that the Day of the Lord comes like a thief in the night, and I wonder why it is that Christmas so often comes like a thief in the night for me.

I remember standing by my mother's side in the kitchen—on a little chrome stool to help me gain counter height—receiving patient instruction on how to form the small, savory meatballs that will be served at our Christmas Eve smorgasbord; how to work the cookie press as we prepare dozen upon dozen buttery spritzes that will melt in the mouth; how to heat the oil "just so" for puffy rosettes, and then dust them with powdered sugar. I can hear the slam of the back door as my father enters the kitchen and gives my mother a hug; she complains that she's behind on the baking, the whole thing has snuck up on her, and he steps back and asks, "What, you weren't expecting Christmas to be on the twenty-fifth this year? You thought maybe it would be later?"

For my observance of Advent is still very much an observance of womanly busy-ness, of being the Swedish mother, the Martha, in the kitchen cooking, in the living room vacuuming, in the bedrooms changing the sheets, in the dining room setting the table. Perhaps this year I can do less. We could decline some of the less important invitations. I could skip the peanut brittle and maybe the gingersnaps. It would still be Christmas if we didn't have those. I could spend a little more time with myself, a little more time with God, and a little less with the Mixmaster.

> *Watch at all times, praying for the strength to stand with confidence before the Son of Man.*

On the second Sunday of Advent I arrive at church having made my seasonal list, having reconciled the various programs and invitations, having done the big shopping trip. And the minister opens the service with:

> *The kingdom of God is close at hand: Repent, and believe the gospel.*

Christmas is close at hand! Holy cow! Only . . . only sixteen more days 'til Christmas. Advent is short this year—always happens when Christmas comes in the middle of the week. I may never get the hang of Advent, I despair. It's not really in my blood. It's not a Baptist sort of concept, really. I was raised in a church that marked the seasons with observances like Valentine's Day Sunday, and Mother's Day Sunday, when we sang "Faith of our Mothers" and an orchid corsage was given to the oldest mother, the mother with the most children present, and the mother who traveled the greatest distance. Or my favorite: Labor Day Sunday. On Labor Day Sunday, my dentist ushered us to our seats in that white smock he wore when he cleaned my teeth, the one that buttoned off-center and had such a high, almost Oriental collar. The farmers wore overalls to church, and women worshipped in housedresses with pretty aprons. Businessmen and teachers looked the way they always did. Memorial Day flowers and special music, Thanksgiving Day prayers, New Year's Eve watchnight services—these comprised the liturgical year of my childhood.

I am struck with free-church panic, the same sort of panic I get when I arrive for worship on Easter realizing that I'm not prepared for the resurrection because I didn't observe Lent. My heart actually starts to thump, and I realize that I'm here, in this holy place, smack dab in the middle of Advent, and I don't have any idea what I'm supposed to be doing about it. What does it mean? What does it mean that the kingdom of God is close at hand? Repent, and believe the gospel—that's what it means.

I fall on my knees and confess my sins. "For the sake of your Son Jesus Christ, who died for us, forgive us all that is past; and grant that we may serve you in newness of life to the glory of your name. Amen," I intone with profound shame. Amen.

How sweet are the words of the Lord to the taste, sweeter than honey to the mouth. Through his precepts we get understanding.

On the third Sunday in Advent:

When the Lord comes, he will bring to light things now hidden in darkness, and will disclose the purposes of the heart.

When the Lord comes. My thoughts are back in time, nine years ago and eleven years ago, when I was waiting for a child to be born. The anticipation! What a frightening, exciting time it was. Every morning I would waken and wonder: is it today? Is this the day when the child will arrive? Is this the day when the child, hidden in my body, will be disclosed to me? When I see his hair, or her toes; his pointy head, her scrawny legs? I wanted so badly to know if I would be mother to a boy or a girl. Would the child be whole? Would it look like me or Steve? My daytime thoughts were hopeful and expectant. But at night I had frightening dreams of deformity and death.

And when it came time for me to be delivered of my children, I was ready. There was no complaining that the babies arrived too soon. By the time my 140 pounds of body weight had become an alarming 185 pounds, by the time my feet had no longer fit into my shoes, by the time I had attended three baby showers . . . I was ready. After checking into the hospital, the examinations, the monitoring, the coaching, the birth itself . . . I was ready. St. Paul had it right when he spoke of the Messiah's coming:

We know that the whole creation has been groaning as in the pains of childbirth right up to the present time.

The scripture is being read, now. "In the wilderness, prepare the way of the Lord, make straight in the desert a highway for our God." And I know that in my heart I am groaning with pain, panting for the kingdom, longing for justice and reconciliation.

Our Lord says, Surely I come quickly. Even so: come, Lord Jesus!

On the fourth Sunday of Advent I stand with the congregation for the introductory sentence:

The glory of the Lord shall be revealed: and all mankind shall see it.

My sons have been shaking the packages already under the Christmas tree. Grandma sent a big box of goodies to our overseas home via air mail—such extravagance! It arrived on Friday: a big, heavy box of toys and books and all manner of heavy gifts, flown from her town in the middle of the United States to our village in Britain. No forward planning, no thought given to cost, no wondering if it's "worth it." Out of the depth of her loving heart she has showered us with large and small gifts, several for each one of us. And now each individually wrapped parcel has found a place under our tree, and the children are wild with excitement. Ross complains of stomach aches and can hardly eat his meals. Drake has nervous legs; his body shakes uncontrollably at the dinner table. They've identified a jigsaw puzzle, and two books—those were easy. Ross was squeezing one small package, and it responded by playing an electronic melody. He and Drake laughed until they cried. A pocket video game! It had to be.

On Christmas morning all will be revealed. There have been hints that we might open gifts—at least one gift?—on Christmas Eve. That's Ross's proposal. But in his heart of hearts he doesn't want a preview. He doesn't want a little bit now and the rest later. He wants it all, in one huge early-morning revelation.

I am sitting on an uncomfortable pew in a church where believers have worshipped since Elizabethan times. In this very spot, men and women of great faith and very little faith have gathered to worship, to pray, to proclaim with their presence that their hope is in the Lord. They, like me, have looked for the glory of the Lord to be revealed.

On this morning we pray for the needs of the world, for we have young men and women preparing for war in a distant land. We pray for the needs of the nation, for there is recession and unemployment and homelessness everywhere. We pray for the needs of our church, for we have a mission to fulfill. And we pray for ourselves, our marriages and our children and our friends. We pray for the glory of the Lord to be revealed.

We are waiting, waiting, for an infinite God, unbound by time and space, to reveal himself to us in a way we can understand.

The virgin is with child and will soon give birth to a son:
and she will call him Emmanuel, God-is-with-us.

On Christmas Eve there is a service of lessons and carols. We begin our worship with a startling promise:

In the morning you shall see the glory of the Lord.

It's all come down to this. All the preparations—the cookies that were made, and the ones that weren't. The presents that were bought, and those that were forgotten. The parties attended, the invitations declined. The cards sent and received, the prayers spoken and unspoken, the days of hectic activity and the quiet evenings staring at the fire. The shops are closed, the readying is over. If it hasn't been done yet, it won't be done at all. In the morning we shall see the glory of the Lord.

In the candlelit silence, eyes closed, I see a clearing. It is a small patch of nothing in particular, just a bit of nothingness in my world of cinnamon bread and carol sheets and damask napkins and pirate Legos. It is noteworthy for being uncluttered, as a small clearing in a deep wood is noteworthy for being without trees. It is a place of calm in my life, an unstructured center where schedules and recipes and deadlines and obligations cannot thrive. It's not much, but for me it's a start.

The uneven ground shall become level, and the rough places a plain.

It is Christmas Eve. I am almost faint with exhaustion and revelation.

The glory of the Lord shall be revealed, and all mankind shall see it.

CHRISTMAS

Eugene H. Peterson

Two years ago at Christmas I was living in Montana in the Rocky Mountains where I grew up. The National Forest Service there allows people to cut their own Christmas tree. So Jan, my wife, and I went out one day with an ax into the snow-filled forest to get ours. We spotted what looked like the right tree—it was 200 yards up a hillside, and we had to tramp through snow to get to it. In that forest and on that hillside it was a spectacularly beautiful tree. But after we got it back to our home on the lake and set it up in our wood-fired and carpeted living room, we realized that a considerable amount of its charm had been lost in transit.

It was an Engleman spruce, a tree with character, having lived a hard life on the mountain, and we had hiked through sixteen inches of snow to get it. It still looked handsome enough to me, but when our three children, all adults now, arrived to celebrate the holiday with us, they took one look and mocked.

They were used to coifed Scotch pines, bought from the Lions Club in the Safeway parking lot in Maryland. If those were too picked over, we patronized the Boy Scouts selling from the Methodist parking lot. Buying a tree was a family affair, with arguments about size and thickness and symmetry. This was our first tree chosen without benefit of children.

In Montana, with an entire forest of trees to pick from, they thought we could have done better. We reminisced about the Christmas trees we had bought and set up and decorated. The more we talked, the more scrawny this Engleman spruce appeared. But finally we all agreed it was a tree, after all, and the moment it was designated "Christmas tree," it was suitable.

People worry these days about keeping Christ in Christmas; no one has any anxiety about keeping the tree in Christmas. Nobody I know discusses the pros and cons of the matter; it is simply done. There must be numerous households in America where no prayers are offered at Christmas, no carols sung, and no nativity story told. But there can be few households where there is no Christmas tree. The tree is required. We always had a tree and always will. It is as much a part of Christmas as the crèche and "Silent Night."

But I do remember a Christmas when there was no tree. I was eight years old. My mother, an intense woman capable

of fierce convictions, was reading the prophecy of Jeremiah
and came upon words she had never noticed before:

> *Thus says the Lord:*
> *"Learn not the way of the nations,*
> *nor be dismayed at the signs of the*
>   *heavens*
> *because the nations are*
>   *dismayed at them,*
> *for the customs of the*
>   *peoples are false.*
> *A tree from the forest is*
> *cut down, and worked*
> *with an ax by the hands*
>   *of a craftsman.*
> *Men deck it with silver and gold;*
>   *they fasten it with ham-*
> *mer and nails so that it*
> *cannot move."* (Jeremiah 10:2–4)

There was no doubt in her mind that the Holy Spirit,
through the prophet Jeremiah, had targeted our American
Christmas in his warning satire. Every detail fit our practice.

A couple of weeks before Christmas, on a Sunday afternoon, my father would get the ax and check its edge. He was
a butcher, used to working with sharp tools, and he did not
tolerate dull edges. When I heard the whetstone applied to
the ax, I knew that the time was near. We bundled into our
Model A Ford pickup, my parents and baby sister and I.

If it was not too cold, I rode in the open truck bed with
our springer spaniel, Brownie, and held the ax. It was a
bouncy ride of ten miles to Lake Blaine, where the Swan

Range of the Rocky Mountains took its precipitous rise from the valley floor. There had been a major forest fire in this region a few years before, so the trees were young—the right size to fit into our living room. I always got to pick the tree; it was a ritual I stretched out as long as parental patience and winter temperatures would accommodate.

My father then took over, swinging the ax. Four or five brisk cuts, and the green-needled spire was horizontal in the snow: *A tree from the forest is cut down.*

He then squared the base of the trunk so it would be easy to mount when we got it back home: *Worked with an ax by the hands of a craftsman.* My father was deft with the ax—the wood chips from the whittling released the fragrance of resin in the winter air.

When we arrived home, I climbed into the attic and handed down the box of decorations. We had multicolored lights on our tree and lots of tinsel. Across the street, my best friends had all blue lights, and I felt sorry for them, stuck with a monochrome Christmas.

My father took slats from packing boxes that our sausage and lunch meats were shipped in—there was always a pile of these boxes in the alley behind our butcher shop—and cut them into four 18-inch supports and nailed them to the tree trunk: *They fasten it with hammer and nails so that it cannot move.*

By now it was late afternoon and dark. Our Douglas fir—it was always a Douglas fir for us, no other evergreen was a Christmas tree—was secure and steady before our living room window, facing the street. We strung the lights, hung the silver and gold ornaments, and draped the tinsel: *Men deck it with silver and gold.*

When we were done, I ran out onto the gravel road (the paving on Fourth Street West fell short by about 400 yards

12

of reaching our house) and looked at it from the outside, the way passersby would see it, the framed picture of our Christmas ritual adventure into and out of the woods. I imagined strangers looking at it and wishing they could be inside with us, part of the ax/Model-A-pickup/Lake Blaine/tree-choosing/tree-cutting/tree-mounting/tree-decorating liturgy that I loved so much.

And I would look across the street at the tree with blue lights where the Mitchell twins, Alva and Alan, lived—so cold and monotonous. They never went to church, and at times like this it showed. I couldn't help feeling privileged and superior, but also a little sorry for them: Christian pride modified by Christian compassion.

And then, in the winter of 1940, when I was eight years old, we didn't have a tree: *For the customs of the peoples are false.* It wasn't just the tree that was absent, the richly nuanced ritual was abolished. A noun, "tree," was deleted from December, but along with it an adjective, "Christmas." Or so I felt.

And it was all because Jeremiah had preached his Christmas Tree Sermon. Because Jeremiah had looked through his prophetic telescope, his spirit-magnified vision reaching across 12,000 miles and 2,600 years saw in detailed focus what we did every December and denounced it as idolatry. And it was because my mother cared far more about Scripture than culture.

I was embarrassed—humiliated was more like it—humiliated as only eight-year-olds can be humiliated. Abased. Mortified. I was terrified of what my friends in the neighborhood would think: They would think we were too poor to have a tree. They would think I was being punished for some unspeakable sin and so deprived of a tree. They would think we didn't care about each other and didn't have any fun in our house. They would feel sorry for us. They would feel superior to us.

As a regular feature of the child-world holiday socializing in our neighborhood, we went to each other's houses, looked at the presents under the trees, wondering what we would get. Every house was so different—I marveled at the odd ways people arranged their furniture. I was uneasy with the vaguely repellent odors in houses where the parents smoked and drank beer. At the Zacharys, three houses down, there was a big pot of moose-meat chili simmering on the back of the wood stove for most of the winter—it was easily the best-smelling house among those of my friends.

But that year, I kept everyone out of our house. I was ashamed to have them come in and see the bare, treeless room. I was terrified of the questions they would ask. I made up excuses to keep them out. I lied: "My sister has a contagious disease"; "My mother is really mad and I can't bring anybody in." But the fact of *no-Christmas-tree* could not be hidden. After all, it was always in our front window.

Alva and Alan, the twins who never went to church, asked the most questions, sensing something wrong, an edge of taunting now in their voices. I made excuses: "My dad is too busy right now; we're planning on going out next week." And on and on.

I was mostly terrified that they would discover the real reason we didn't have a tree: that God had commanded it (at least we thought so at the time)—a religious reason! But religion was the one thing that made us better than our neighbors; and now, if they were to find out our secret, it would make us worse!

My mother read Jeremiah to me and my little sister that year and talked about Jesus. She opened the Bible to the story of the nativity and placed it on the table where the Christmas tree always stood. I never told her how I felt or what I knew everyone in the neighborhood was saying. I carried my humiliation secretly, as children often do, stoical in the uncomprehending adult world.

It is odd when I think back on it now, but we never went to church on Christmas. Every detail of our lives was permeated with an awareness of God. There was a rigorous determination to let Scripture and Christ shape not only our morals and worship but also the way we used language and wore our clothes. Going to church was the act that pivoted the week. But there was no church-going on Christmas.

On Christmas Eve we exchanged and opened presents; on Christmas Day we had a dinner at our house with a lot of relatives in attendance, plus any loose people in the neighborhood—bachelors, widows, runaways.

Christmas dinner was full of Norwegian talk. It was the only day in the year I heard Norwegian spoken. My uncles and aunts reminisced over their Norway Christmases and savored the sounds of their cradle tongue. The Christmas menu was always the same: *lutefisk*, fish with all the taste and nutrients leached out of it by weeks of baptism in barrels of brine, and *lefsa*, an unleavened, pliable flat bread with the texture (and taste) of a chamois cloth.

There was a stout but unsuccessful attempt to restore flavor by providing great bowls of melted butter, salt cellars, and much sugar. It was a meal I never learned to like. But I loved the festivities—the stories in Norwegian that I couldn't understand, the laughter, the fun, the banter.

The primary source of the banter was my favorite uncle. He was the best storyteller and always seemed to have the most fun. He also posed as an atheist (I think it was a pose), which provoked my mother, on alternate days, to prayer and indignation. On the Christmas we had no tree, he surpassed himself in banter.

He was the first to remark its absence: "Evelyn," he roared at my mother, "where the hell is the Christmas tree? How the hell are we going to celebrate a Norwegian Christmas without a tree?" (He was also the only person I ever heard use profanity in our home, which set him apart in my child mind on a sort of craggy eminence.) My mother's reply, a nice fusion of prayer and indignation, was a match to his raillery: "Brother, we are not celebrating a Norwegian Christmas this year; we are celebrating a Christian Christmas." Then she got out Jeremiah and read it to him. He was astonished. He had no idea that anything that tellingly contemporary could come out of an old-fashioned Bible. He was silenced, if only briefly.

The next year we had a Christmas tree. The entire ritual was back in place without explanation. Our gray and rust Model A was replaced by a red Dodge half-ton, but that was the only change. I never learned what authority preempted Jeremiah in the matter of the Christmas tree. Years later my mother occasionally said, "Eugene, do you remember that silliness about the Christmas tree when you were eight years old?" I didn't want to remember, and we didn't discuss it.

But now I want to remember. And I want to discuss it. It doesn't seem at all silly now. My mother died four years ago, and so I am not going to find out the details that interest me—the turns and twists of pilgrimage during those years when she was so passionate in pursuit of a holy life. She may have been wise in restoring the tree to our Christmas celebrations, but I am quite sure that it was not silliness that banned it that single year.

The feelings I had that Christmas when I was eight years old may have been the most authentically Christmas feelings I have ever had, or will have: the experience of humiliation, of being misunderstood, of being an outsider. Mary was pregnant out of wedlock. Joseph was an apparent cuckold. Jesus was born in poverty. God had commanded a strange word; the people in the story were aware, deeply and awesomely aware, that the event they were living was counter to the culture and issued from the Spirit's power.

They certainly experienced considerable embarrassment and inconvenience—did they also clumsily lie to their friends and make excuses at the same time they persisted in faith? All the joy and celebration and gift-receiving in the gospel nativity story took place in a context of incomprehension and absurdity. Great love was given and received and celebrated, a glorious festivity, but the neighborhood was not in on it, and the taunts and banter must have cut cruelly into their spirits.

So, Mother, thank you. And don't apologize for the silliness. Thank you for providing me with a taste of the humiliation that comes from pursuing a passionate conviction in Christ. Thank you for introducing into my spirit a seed of discontent with all cultural displays of religion, a seed that has since grown tree-sized. Thank you for being relaxed in grace and reckless enough to risk a mistake. Thank you for being scornful of caution and careless of opinion. Thank you for training me in discernments that in adult years have been a shield against the seduction of culture-religion. Thank you for the courage to give me Jesus without tinsel, embarrassing as it was for me (and also for you?).

Thank you for taking away the Christmas tree the winter I was eight years old. And thank you for giving it back the next year.

ST. STEPHEN, FIRST MARTYR

❦

Harold Fickett

Martyrs have always made me nervous. When I think of martyrdom, I think first of the missionaries who used to come speak to our church when I was a boy. I remember sitting in the back pews of the balcony during my junior high years, high up above the missionary speaker so that I stared down at the crown of his head and the wedge of his nose. His tales of martyrdom competed for my attention with the shining-haired nymphet next to me, with her white lipstick and empire-waisted dress, its tight cinch underlining her upturned breasts.

The speaker was usually a missionary from the Ivory Coast or from what was known then as the Belgian Congo in Africa—Africa being the venue of choice in those days for martyrdom. He nearly always told the story of a premier student in the missionary church school, a stunningly bright young man who had tramped out from the interior. He was always admitted to the school, despite the lack of space, because he had camped out on the missionaries' doorstep, day after day, and simply refused to leave.

One day the Rebels would come and round up this student, Kitongo, and his friends and keep them stashed in a village of abandoned huts further on in the interior. Kitongo and friends begin to sing the songs the missionaries taught them, African versions of "Nearer My God to Thee" and the like, right up until the last moment when they are toppled back into their mass grave by the bullets blowing through their chests.

Later, one of the executioners would steal to the missionaries' door and ask how Kitongo and his friends could have died so happily.

My hands would be cold, white, and numb as I examined my conscience, at the missionary's directions, as to whether, seated here in this plush sanctuary, in the all-too-comfortable and free U.S.A., I would be willing to die for my faith. I always tried to summon up the courage to believe that under certain circumstances, given a prevailing tail wind of group encouragement, yes, you bet your love offering I would. I never really believed in my bravado. I would not have expressed it this way at the time, but my sentiments ran to *Good Lord, deliver us.* The nymphet at my side would always look at me earnestly, a deep, deep appreciation of the erotic attraction of death pouring through her eyes, and at that I would really feel ill. Sometimes I went forward during the subsequent altar call to commit myself to full-time Christian service with an ambivalence so keen I was probably in a clinically dissociated state.

So the irony that now in my adult life I use a Catholic breviary as the basis of my own prayers, and these prayers celebrate, on feast day after feast day, the celebrated martyrs of the Church, starting with the protomartyr, St. Stephen, causes me to wonder. Do I wish to have anything more to do with this company of St. Stephen, St. Polycarp, St. Sebastian, St. Agnes, St. Fabian, St. Vincent, St. Blase, etc., then I did with St. Kitongo?

One of the most important books in my life has been Graham Greene's *The Power and the Glory*. Oddly enough, it's a martyr's story as well, the story of the "whiskey priest," who stumbles through a revolutionary Mexican landscape doing his duty, being a priest, despite his own fears and his unworthiness. Greene provides a counterpoint to the story of the whiskey priest in that of "young Juan," the hero of a pious book that a Catholic mother reads to her children. Young Juan is Kitongo in a serape. The good schoolboy, the model seminarian, the compassionate village priest. He dies before the firing squad with his hands raised, shouting, *¡Viva el Cristo Rey!* Long live Christ the King!

The young boy in the family who listens to his mother reading this story finds young Juan disgusting. (My honest reaction to Kitongo, exactly.) But a brush with the whiskey priest fascinates the boy and turns his sympathies against the revolutionaries and toward the church.

Greene's whiskey priest performed this same function in my life. Here was a spirituality I could believe in. The whiskey priest does not know whether what he is doing makes any sense; he does know he is not worthy of doing it, and he suspects that Christ must have abandoned him long ago to his own lusts and appetites. To his craving for brandy, if nothing else. (Vicariously, to my lust for the shining nymphet.) Yet he keeps on. And when he dies, although his legs won't stay under him, he burbles out the appropriate exclamation: Long live Christ the King!

I think that much of the way we talk about spiritual experience is highly misleading: the "sweeter-as-the-days-go-by" terminology of the past led me to suspect that if people really felt about God the way they said, then I knew nothing of God. Greene's whiskey priest helped me to understand that the things of the spirit are grounded in the humdrum aspects of who we are and how we feel.

I am afraid of death. I bet you are too.

Ernest Becker, in what I think will prove one of the lasting works of psychology, *The Denial of Death*, argues persuasively that a universal fear of death gives rise to the way in which we construct our personalities. Our personalities represent a working lie about our last end, when they work; and when they stop working it is often because we lose the sense of the lie and start believing in our own godlike invincibility. That's one way of talking about pride or original sin: the death-in-life we experience.

Walker Percy says that we all arrive on this earth and wake up to the fact that we are desperately in need of *news* as to our dilemma: we are self-consciously mortal creatures with self-consciously immortal longings. What to do?

Remember O man, says the prophet, from dust thou art and to dust thou shalt return. Not on your life, we say.

And yet besides celebrating the feast days of the martyrs, there are other daily *memento mori*; at least there are if you have reached any age beyond twenty-five. I don't need to keep a skull on my desk like St. Jerome to consider my last end. My hair falling out, my gums bleeding, my gut expanding, and my muscles atrophying, all these prompt the recollection of the grave. I always think I am going to wake up one day and see my true self in the mirror again—but no.

It turns out that martyrdom is not an elective procedure. Well, martyrdom may still be, but death certainly isn't. We have no choice about death. We are going to die. I am going to die. As Tolstoy put it, a corpse is unanswerable.

What do I do then with all my fear and anxiety about death? What do I do with my longings for some other fate? And how do I receive the advance heralds of the grim reaper: plans that go awry, friendships that break apart, aging. Who will deliver me from the body of this death?

Consider the martyrs. Consider St. Stephen. In the midst of his persecutors, he gazed into heaven and "saw the glory of God, and Jesus standing at God's right hand." I am not sure what we are to make of this, but being of a medieval turn of mind, I may try to allegorize it.

St. Stephen was a sort of super-spiritual smart aleck. When he was put on trial before the Sanhedrin, he reprised for them the entire history of the Jews, with special emphasis on how the people had always killed their prophets. He was asking for it. And his persecutors obliged. He also prayed that his persecutors would be forgiven, an act of contrition that meets the reciprocal standards of the Lord's prayer: forgive us as we forgive others. He cannot, finally, be faulted for provocation, and his readiness to go into eternity may have caused the Lord to receive him so eagerly.

We, too, it seems to me, have to be ready to "ask for it"—to ask for our deaths. That is, when it comes to death, our only choice seems to be how we predispose ourselves to receive it. If we give up our lives, if we override the most fundamental drive of who we are as creatures, the will to survive, with the conscious decision to acknowledge God as the ruler of our lives, then he may, as he has promised, return to us that life in heaven. I am a great doubter, but there is always one verse in Scripture that holds me on this score. In my house there are many mansions, Christ says; if it were not so I would have told you. That always makes me cry. That's my hope. And I am staking a lot on this one.

Or at least I seem to be. What is death otherwise? An event whose meaning consists in its lack of meaning, the end it puts to meaning. I suppose we can think of finding a meaning in rebellion, not going gentle into that good night but howling against the darkness. But what would this signify? Who is there to care? In my end is my beginning, as Eliot quotes Mary, Queen of Scots; my death makes way for a new beginning. Or in my end is—very strictly speaking—nothing. The Christian response to death, the putting of one's life at God's disposal, seems to be called for by the nature of the event itself; the one meaning it suggests, if it suggests any at all.

The strangest thing about St. Stephen's feast day is that it is celebrated the day after Christmas. The long-awaited Birth; Good tidings of great joy! the angels cry; and then, bang, death, martyrdom. One moment we are shouting hosanna and the next we are climbing into our coffins for a reflective pause. Why this near conjunction?

T. S. Eliot's poem, "Journey of the Magi," contains the brooding spirit demanded by a feast day like St. Stephen's that teaches us how quickly death follows on the heels of birth. At the end of the poem, the wise man who is remembering his journey to see the Christ Child says he'll be glad to meet death. He is no longer at ease among what he now considers a pagan people, in the "old dispensation," and he tells us that he has seen both death and life, but before his visit to Judea, he thought these were different. But the meaning of the Christ child's birth for this wise man, and the meaning of a martyr's feast day coming on the day after Christmas for us, comes to be about how we must live as dying creatures. We have to embrace death. We have to greet death with gladness, although everything in us pleads with us to deny its reality. That is the only good news capable of assuaging our fears.

In the prayers of the people for St. Stephen's Day, we pray for the freedom of the Spirit, faith that is constant and pure, the ability to endure courageously the misfortunes of life, and God's help in avoiding the weaknesses of the flesh and worldly allurements. We pray that our daily struggles, our ongoing martyrdom, will teach us how to renounce our own sovereignty and enable us to deliver our spirit into the Lord's hands. This is not something junior high kids generally know how to do—although they already are being exposed to shining nymphets and other "allurements of the flesh." This is not something I know how to do now as the signs of my mortality become more evident, nor am I particularly eager to learn these lessons.

But the test awaits. The test is inevitable. And so, not only *Good Lord, deliver us*, but *St. Stephen, pray for us*, as well.

HOLY INNOCENTS

William Griffin

"All the babies prevented by the pill showed up," droned Steven Wright, recalling a bad dream in one of his comedy routines; "were they mad!"

To obtain my minimum daily requirement of comedy, I often turn to cable television's Comedy Channel. There, one day, on SAST ("Short Attention Span Theatre"), I discovered Wright, whose routines are composed of strings of improbable ironies, chains made not of daisies but of poisonous orchids; his delivery is comatose, but his comic observations often hit the mark.

Wildly improbable as his phantasm about the waiting

babies was, it did generate another image and another irony in my imagination.

"I had a bad dream last night"—this is what I would say in a caustic comedy routine like Wright's. "All the babies conceived by their parents, but done in by abortionists, showed up, and were they hopping mad!!!"

What has this madness in heaven got to do with the Holy Innocents, the babes in Nazareth who lost their lives that the baby Jesus might live?

A great deal, really, but perhaps it's better to begin at the beginning.

From the magi, the wandering astrologers, Herod the Great, the reigning monarch of Judea, had heard a rumor that the king of the Jews had been born. Afraid that he'd be bumped from the throne, which he had maintained for decades by systematically assassinating his relatives, he ordered the slaughter of all babies under two years of age, or so the evangelist Matthew has recorded (2:16–18); it is a brief mention and indeed the only mention in the Gospels. Why the age of two? The mad Idumean, it seemed, had grilled the magi, learned their astrological calculations, and accessing his abacus, finally determined that the new king of the Jews, if such a tot had been born, could be no more than two years of age, and sent his hairy men to do the dirty deed. It's a gruesome event to contemplate in the mind, but on the big screen it is almost unbearable. In Pier Paolo Pasolini's *The Gospel According to Saint Matthew*, it was portrayed by horsemen galloping about Nazareth; mothers wrestled with the soldiers for possession of their babies, but in the end the poor women lost.

How many died that day? Scholars have not distinguished themselves in ascertaining the number. In Justin Martyr's *Dialogues*, Herod was described as having ordered the slaughter of all the boys without mention of age limit. The Byzantine liturgy set the number of infants at 14,000; Syrian menologies or calendars of saints put it at 64,000; and by accommodation with Revelation 14:1–5, the number has reached even 144,000.

Contemporary scholar Raymond Brown has developed a hypothesis: if the population were 1,000, if there were a high mortality rate, and if the annual birth rate were thirty, the male children under two years of age would scarcely have numbered more than twenty. And of course there are other scholars, W. F. Albright and C. S. Mann among them, who think that the population of Bethlehem was only 300, and that the flayed infants numbered from twenty-five to as few as six. That would make it, in the grand scale of Herod's atrocities, a minor incident. But I would double that number—from twelve to twenty-four to perhaps as many as fifty—for how a soldier, in the hurly-burly of hacking a mewling and puking infant to death could tell whether that tot was under, and not over, two years of age—the mothers were surely of no help here—stretches the imagination.

When the horsemen departed, the moaning and mourning that rose from the village could be heard, or so the evangelist would have us believe, in Rama, five miles as the sparrow flies. Thus was fulfilled—Matthew here providing a literary echo to an older Scripture—what had been spoken by the prophet Jeremiah:

A voice was heard in Rama,
weeping and loud mourning,

> *Rachel crying for her children;*
> *and she would not be consoled,*
> *because they were no more.*

From the first, the infants were considered to be martyrs because they died not only for Christ but also instead of Christ. Remembrance of their sacrifice has been kept in the West from the fourth century of the Christian era. In the Martyrology of Jerome they were called "the holy babes and sucklings"; in the Calendar of Carthage, simply "the infants"; in the East "the holy children"; in the West, "the holy innocents." In the fifth century, St. Augustine described them as *flores martyrum,* buds killed by the frost of persecution the moment they showed themselves. Not inappropriately, the liturgical feast day in England was for centuries called Childermas. In the West it is commemorated on December 28; in the East, on December 29.

"In honoring the Innocents," writes David Hugh Farmer in his *Oxford Dictionary of Saints,* "the Church honors all who die in a state of innocence and consoles parents of dead children with the conviction that these also will share the glory of the infant companions of the infant Jesus."

Which brings me back to where I began. What has this madness in heaven—the babies in waiting—got to do with the Holy Innocents, the babes in Nazareth who lost their lives that the baby Jesus might live?

I can answer only with another question.

Why has no one, especially in the week between Christmas and New Year's, made a connection—rhetorical or even metaphorical—between those boys in Nazareth two thousand years ago who tasted the sword and those babes since *Roe v. Wade* (1973) who've choked on the salt?

It's a poetic, not a logical, leap that makes this connection, but since the church that commemorates the sacrifice of the Holy Innocents is also the church that condemns abortion, such a hop, skip, and jump would seem to be an easy one . . . except if one is an ethicist. Some there are in the church who hold that abortion is not unchoosable in each and every situation.

I was reminded of this by the recent death of a family friend, the Jesuit priest who presided at our marriage. He was a philosopher of some renown, albeit in a small circle, who had so developed his sensitivity to logic that it became like a gold leaf fluttering at the least ratiocination. Long ago he had decided that since medical science couldn't pinpoint when personhood, let alone when soulhood, entered the embryo or fetus, then philosophy in general, and logic in particular, could not stand in the way of medical science when it wanted to have its way with tissue living *in utero*.

But I, with a metaphorical eye, can see what the philosopher-theologian sometimes can't. I can see clearly at high noon what Steven Wright saw dreamily at midnight: babies, bevies of babies, unborn and unbegot. The unbegot are sitting about on a grassy knoll, with no clothes on and nowhere special to go. The begotten but not-yet-born are all dressed up and indeed have somewhere very definite to go. They're wearing navy blue coats with gold buttons, probably double-breasted, with shorts, knee socks, and peaked caps over golden locks; that's what my mother thought the best-dressed Celtic tugger should wear when I was a boy, the sort of outfit sold by Best's, whose store in Brookline, Massachusetts, then boasted a monochromatic mural, probably brown on beige, of a variety of little creatures capering about a giant, drawn from *Gulliver's Travels*; the children's department was called "The Lilliputian Bazaar"; it was a marvel of merchandising.

Neither the unborn nor the unbegot seem to talk with each other, nor do they titter or chuckle, skip rope or play hopscotch. They are toyless and indeed joyless. On the face of each is an anxious, worried expression, the forehead so fresh that it can't even furrow. They'd chew their nails if they had any, afraid that they're standing at the wrong bus stop, waiting at the wrong train station, sweating it out at the wrong airport. For the unborn are fearful that, although they received a friendly invitation, no friend will come for them, afraid finally that they will die before they're born.

Much as the ululation rose in Herod's time, it rises today when pro-choicers and pro-lifers encounter each other on platforms and at street corners. The joy of witness buoys both sides; they exult in the rightness of their positions; then there is the joy of combat, verbal and eventually physical. Sniveling begets scuffling, and the larger the crowd, the more dangerous the collision. When the smoke rises and the site clears, there lies, trampled to death in the street, Lady Charity, the mother of all virtues . . . but will anyone lament her passing? Whatever the Supreme Court finally says about the legality, if not the morality, of abortion, the loser will have to live with the winner, and wouldn't it be a shame if neither could talk charitably with the other? For if charity is not the *lingua franca* among the living, then I daresay that the legions of holy innocents who've perished by virtue of *Roe v. Wade* have died in vain.

In conclusion, what are we to think of the holy innocents, then and now? They await the general resurrection like the rest of us, I'd like to imagine, but they do their waiting in a sort of limbo, perhaps not unlike a doll hospital or teddy bear factory. At the final assembly the innocents of old will get a good brushing to brighten up their nap, with perhaps some new eyes and whiskers. The innocents from anew, those that were dismembered anyway, will be put right again. At the final trump of the toy soldiers, all the limbs will be rejoined to the proper trunks, and all the heads will be snapped onto the proper shoulders. Everything will be velvet and velour once again!

THE SOLEMNITY OF MARY

Emilie Griffin

Now a great sign appeared in heaven: a woman, robed with the sun, standing on the moon, and on her head a crown of twelve stars. She was pregnant, and in labor, crying aloud in the pangs of childbirth. (Revelation 12:1–3)

This birthing that the Book of Revelation describes in high poetic language is the birthing we commemorate (though sometimes in lackluster fashion) on January first in the Solemnity of Mary as the Mother of God. Drifting into our consciousness somewhere between our awareness of Christmas parties, the frenzied observance of New Year's Eve and the intense football competitions and pageants that sweep us up on New Year's afternoon, the Solemnity of Mary almost disappears in the Christmas season as nothing more than a vague remembrance of ancient devotion. . . . Or is it, can it somehow be, more? What we need to snap us out of our vague reveries on the morning of January 1 is the highly charged apocalyptic of the Sun-Clothed Woman:

> *Then a second sign appeared in the sky: there was a huge red dragon with seven heads and ten horns, and each of the heads crowned with a coronet. Its tail swept a third of the stars from the sky and hurled them to the ground, and the dragon stopped in front of the woman as she was at the point of giving birth, so that he could eat the child as soon as it was born . . . (12:3–5)*

What a cosmic drama! The spiritually exalted Sky-Mother, robed in prophetic power, bears within her womb the Child who is to transform the world.

> *The woman was delivered of a boy, the son who is to rule all the nations with an iron sceptre, and the child was taken straight up to God and to his throne. (12:5–6)*

In the strong, savage imagery of this primitive book, the story of our salvation is being painted in bold allegorical terms. But can our modern imaginations surrender entirely to the drama of the transcendent Woman, bearing salvation in her womb? Can we nowadays accept the notion of salvation as angelic warfare, a clash between Good and Evil, not to mention the unleashed energies of masculine and feminine archetypes?

This imaginative show of spiritual fireworks spread out across an apocalyptic sky is the representation of God-Power in highly creative terms. And I believe this is the Mary that the Church wants to hold up for us when we contemplate Mary as the God-Bearer, giving birth to Christ's saving power in our lives. And yes, I think this depiction of a world in conflict between the power of God and the relentless on-slaught of evil is entirely topical and pertinent to world events most days of the week. But we moderns are suffering from a weakening of poetic and imaginative courage. We have had our religious imaginations deflated, somehow, by the spiritual impoverishment of our times. We need a new burst of religious and literary daring—one that allows us to connect our experience to the dazzling metaphors of Scripture. And in this particular feast, on January first, we have a superb opportunity, because this feast is a pure dogma, an enflesh-ment of the high theological drama of God surrendering to the tiny space of the womb.

As one twentieth-century writer expressed it, the dogma *is* the drama. Dorothy L. Sayers, wit, scholar, theologian, novelist and playwright, is one who believed that the harsh and compelling metaphors of a high Christology and a high orthodoxy could still take hold of the modern imagination. She was constantly distressed by contemporary efforts to make Christianity palatable and relevant. Most of all, she understood that even the formulations of the Creed are essen-tially dramatic. The story of the incarnation, of salvation and redemption, must be acted out passionately on the inner stage of our imagination. Yet this view is neither literalist nor fundamentalist; it is a sophisticated faith-surrender.

Blessed art thou among women; and blessed is the fruit of thy womb, Jesus.

When imagination is shaken from its lethargy, this New Year's feast offers us a real chance to contemplate the baffling mystery at the center of our religion, how God became not only a man, but first a child, and before a child a fetus, and before that, an embryo, even before that a fuzzy, floating presence in the womb we call a zygote or a blastocyst; took part entirely in the mystery of human existence; in defiance of all common sense and practicality, the God who rules existence became us, and was carried for nine months in the dark space of a woman's body, till he was born in some obscure country place in the Middle East known as Bethlehem. Can we grasp this? Can we seize it, make it ours? Can we really entertain the idea that God has a mother? Can we open up to the seeming impossibility our ancient theological formula demands of us?

Even when we begin to be wounded by the piercing beauty of this salvation-imagery, something inside us holds back, a little voice keeps nagging away. What in the world, it inquires, does any of this time-honored tableau of salvation have to do with the way we live now? What does this exalted Virgin, in her royal cloth of gold, actually demand of us? What lessons does she come to teach? When the exquisite vision fades, won't we be left somewhat confused and alienated, in the half-light of our workaday lives? Isn't Mary-the-Mother-of-God mostly a high medieval entertainment to keep us peasants happy on feast days so we'll work more contentedly during the rest of the week?

In answer to this Thomas-doubt, words of Scripture leap to mind:

> *And it happened that as he was speaking, a woman in*
> *the crowd raised her voice and said, "Blessed is the womb*
> *that bore you and the breasts that fed you!" But [Jesus]*
> *replied, "More blessed still are those who hear the word*
> *of God and keep it."* (Luke 11:27–28)

This saying of Jesus reminds us of how things really are. What has been nurtured in Mary's womb is our fertility; what Mary has labored to give birth to is the Christ who rules in us. We are somehow the womb, the rich creative environment in which Christ's meaning can take hold, be nourished in dark spaces, grow and swell, breaking open at last in ways that can invigorate our lives.

We have heard, endlessly and wearisomely, all the countless reasons why Mary "doesn't work" as a metaphor for our times and for our generation. We have heard the whimpers and the cries of rage, the anger and disillusionment; we have heard that Mary is too passive, too much of a people-pleaser; too weak, too virginal, too pure, too easily shaped, too obedient, too good to be true. All these complaints seem thin, and beside the point, when we contemplate the poetic simplicity of her girlish form, bending with tenderness over the child in the hay; when we experience the revolutionary power of her appearance among the poor and the oppressed; when we take into account her constant willingness to appear to simple folk in unlikely places, leaving behind her the waters of healing springs and roses that last on shawls for centuries; and when we hear her voice speaking (we don't know precisely how) in the inner reaches of our hearts, asking us to pray for the conversion of whole countries and continents, warning us to prepare for apocalyptic events; calling us, always, into the childlike simplicity we knew long ago when we lined up in rows to be shepherds and wise men, when we wove flowers and branches into May-crowns for pageants.

"Immensity, cloistered in thy dear womb," wrote the seventeenth-century poet-priest John Donne in his sonnet on the Annunciation. His characteristic skill at capturing a dogma in a mystic's metaphor reminds us of the great gift to devotion that is offered by creative artists. In earlier centuries, Christian poets, storytellers and playwrights added constantly to the wealth of material that could be drawn on for devotion; they wove new cloth for our contemplation and prayer. Something much like that is needed for our contemporary imagination now. By grace we can experience a comparable flowering of religious and spiritual imagination, not only for creative artists, but in the depths of our own hearts. Yes, we moderns are capable of a new kind of relationship to Mary, one with a level of sophistication that corresponds to our new Biblical and philosophical understanding. Even for people like us, who have been everywhere and done everything, who have heard and seen it all, it is possible to discover Mary by all her many titles, shedding graces in our Christian lives. What counts is the wanting to, the yielding up of self, the humbling of a particularly contemporary kind of pride.

We need to let go and give way to childlike gifts of spiritual creativity. We need to surrender playfully to our own intuitive and inventive selves. Not all of us have the skill of poets, but within us all is a childlike spiritual sensitivity. Simplicity of heart is the grace we need, a willingness to re-dream the Virgin and, with Mary as the model of our action and contemplation, to set out daringly on a bold adventure of heart and spirit, a work of courage in behalf of peace and reconciliation, of world-transformation, a work of prayer and good works that will let Jesus Christ (it is T. S. Eliot's phrase) redeem the time.

In the words of T. S. Eliot's poem, "Ash Wednesday," the figure of Mary walks prophetically, calling us again to devotion and prayer. She is "one who moves in time between sleep and waking, wearing/White light folded, sheathed about her, folded." How striking the words that follow!

The new years walk, restoring
Through a bright cloud of tears, the years, restoring
With a new verse the ancient rhyme. Redeem
The time. Redeem
The unread vision in the higher dream . . .

When I read the words of Eliot aloud, when I ponder them in my heart, I hear the sound of Mary calling me to prayer; I see the image of a Lady walking through the garden of my heart, the silken sound of her garment an invitation to contemplation and peace; and this Mary that I hear and see is not only the Mary of my thought, but the Mary whom the people have raised up through centuries of devotion, and the Mary who is present in our liturgies and our hillsides wherever Christ is present in our hopes and in our hearts.

And I, Emilie, would find it possible to write (for I seem to hear the prophet saying):

Now a great sign appeared on earth: the sign of the figure
of Mary the Mother of Jesus, Mother of God. And the
creative spirit of the Church, nurtured in her womb, came
forth in a great birth of consciousness. And the hearts of
the people were moved. And they came to understand
that the work of Christian devotion is a work of the

contemporary imagination, placed obediently in the service of God.

Now I, Emilie, hear a new scripture being written in my heart:

And the people were moved and listened to their own hearts speaking. And they understood that the children of God are the children of a royal line, a priesthood set apart. And that each one is holy.

And the figure of Mary the Mother of God was exalted as a sign of the ingathering of the people of God; and there was a great outpouring of understanding and of prayer.

And the people of the new Israel understood that God is doing a new work in our time; and they came to know that our age is part of the new age of Christ, in which existence has already been transformed and all things are coming together for good for those that love God. And they understand with the Holy Mother it is possible to give birth to Christ in our hearts, daily, hourly, in our new year's walk and throughout the Christian year.

One could say that in this reflection on the Solemnity of Mary it is possible to experience still another epiphany, a disclosure of God's grace spilling generously into our lives. And the Gospel for this feast is most fitting:

And Mary kept all these things and pondered them in her heart. (Luke 2:19–20)

EPIPHANY

Luci Shaw

When a real epiphany comes for me, I recognize it as God dealing with me in a direct, irrefutable way. One such sighting came in the fall of 1988. I was teaching poetry at Regent College in Vancouver, Canada, while living an hour away, in Bellingham, Washington.

The Pacific Northwest is known for its rains that fall steadily for days (or weeks) and for clouds that hug the earth, shrouding the landscape in a gentle gloom. Just a few miles in from the coast rise the Cascade Mountains and, spectacular among them, Mt. Baker.

I wrote in my journal:

For weeks I've driven my highway, sixty miles north in the morning, then south again at the end of the day. The mountains are clearly marked on the map, but they might as well not exist, lost as they are in clouds, obscured by drizzle, fog, haze. Then, some morning, unexpectedly, a strong air from the sea will lick away the fog and allow the sun to shine cleanly. And Mt. Baker, towering magnificently beyond the foothills, unbelievably high above the other mountains, is seen to be what it has been all along—immense, serene, unmovable, its dazzling, snow-draped profile cut clear against a sky of jewel blue.

Today it happened. The mountain "came out"! I kept turning my eyes from the highway to look once more at its splendor, wanting to be overwhelmed again and again. It is heart-stopping. I can't get enough of it. And I can never take it for granted—I may not see it again for weeks.

It's God, showing me a metaphor of himself. I mean—he's there, whether I see him or not. It's almost as if he's lying in wait to surprise me. And the wind is like the Spirit, sweeping away my foggy doubt, opening my eyes, revealing the reality of God. Annie Dillard's words say it for me: "It was less like seeing than being for the first time seen, knocked breathless by a powerful glance . . ."

The word *epiphany* means, literally, *a showing.* Traditionally, this showing is accompanied by light; we need light in order to see what is being shown us. And light is something that every human heart longs for and responds to. Day holds all the clarity of brilliance and vision—a certainty, where night brings blindness in the unknowing dark.

Jesus himself was personified as the Sun of righteousness. Even in our diurnal rhythms, day/night/day, sunset is a figure of chill, aging and death, while the appearance of the morning sun over the horizon's blackness speaks of warm hope. This response is so universal that when God explains himself to us in Scripture as light—the "true Light that lightens everyone"—we recognize the glory and joy of the image.

In liturgical churches, the Feast of the Epiphany is the first feast in the calendar New Year. Traditionally it falls on January 6 and celebrates the "showing" of the infant Christ to the Eastern sages in Bethlehem, where they had been led, curiously enough, by a star—a small, glowing, celestial flashlight for their dark path from the Orient. The star of Bethlehem is to me a remote spark from the universal Light toward whom the Wise Men were traveling, a coal from the blaze that sprang up when God struck his match in the world.

This event, the Manifestation of Jesus to the Wise Men, is the sighting of God in the flesh, an event the church has seized upon that lights up the first week of our dark, wintry New Year. But it is not the only one. Often, at the most unexpected moments, Scripture—and life—brings into our focus other sets of sightings, or epiphanies. Perhaps every miracle that Jesus did, every healing, every teaching, was a new showing of himself.

Jesus said, "Blessed are the pure in heart, for they shall see God." This means that as humans are purged and rinsed clean, as they grow more transparent, so that their souls are like windows, they are invited into deeper seeings of God, appearings that have often been terrible—that is, full of terror. Think of Moses on Sinai, of Daniel in Babylon, or of

John on Patmos confronted with the blazing glory of the One like the Son of Man. Think of the series of fearsome sightings in the early chapters of Luke, when the admonition "Don't be afraid" was an assurance badly needed by each of those confronted with a heavenly visitation—Zechariah, Mary, the shepherds.

Though the sudden, dazzling presence of God has often seemed a fearful thing for the humans involved, it has always been what I most dearly long for. God has sometimes disclosed himself to me in ways that I can only call indirect, through metaphors from life and nature and the Bible, through moments with a sense of significance about them, when everything suddenly danced into place. The inexplicable exhilaration of those rare instants redeemed, for a time, my days of chaos and confusion. C. S. Lewis's poem "The Day with a White Mark" says it compellingly:

> *All day I have been tossed and whirled in a preposterous*
> *   happiness;*
> *Was it an elf in the blood? or a bird in the brain? or even*
> *   part*
> *Of the cloudily crested, fifty-league-long, loud uplifted wave*
> *Of a journeying angel's transit roaring over and through my*
> *   heart? . . .*
>
> *. . . the color of my day was like a peacock's chest . . .*
>
> *Who knows if ever it will come again, now the day closes?*
> *No-one can give me, or take away, that key. All depends*
> *On the elf, the bird or the angel. I doubt if the angel*
> *   himself*
> *Is free to choose when sudden heaven in man begins or ends.*

And it's not difficult to remember or experience, with our baptized intellects or imaginations, times of new understanding *about* the Almighty. The Bible is full of metaphors that reveal God in images such as a rock, a banner, a mother hen, a lover, an artist. But all too often I have felt in the dark about God himself—unable to see *him*. Even though Jesus came close to us in the Incarnation, it all seems so long ago. I long for the immediate, unmistakable knowledge of his presence now, the smell, the sight, the touch of him. Even though it might scorch me, such "hard evidence" wouldn't be too hard for me to take.

I have often felt like the three disciples climbing down from Mount Tabor after the Transfiguration, unable to see ahead through the mist that covered the mountain after Jesus appeared to them. Sometimes, in the days following my husband's death, when life was very dark indeed, other people would come to me with stories of their dreams or visions of Harold, which seemed to them like epiphanies. Paula D'Arcy saw him among the worshippers on her church balcony on All Saints' Day, "beaming with light and joy," as she expressed it to me in a phone call.

My friend Georgia Bosch dreamed that she and her husband were eating dinner at our house, and after helping me in the kitchen she re-entered the dining room to see Harold sitting at the head of the table. "Luci thinks she's all alone," he told her, "but I'm watching, and I know everything she does." Margaret Smith has often *heard* God's plans and purposes for me in prayer. These have been comforting assurances, but at a remove, circuitous, second hand, not direct enough to satisfy me. Why didn't the Lord give *me* a vision? Why couldn't I, in the mountaintop sun with Peter, James, and John, see Jesus with his face shining "like the sun, and his clothes dazzling white as light"?

Both by nature and definition, epiphanies of the divine are rare. Exceptional. That is one way we recognize them for what they are. Like miracles, they are not part of the normal fabric of our lives. And they are nearly always individual rather than corporate experiences, personal rather than public spectacles. We cannot participate in the Angel's announcement of the Incarnation to Mary except in imagination. Paul, going to Damascus, was felled to the ground when the flash of light from heaven surrounded him, but those traveling with him saw nothing. And when someone today tells us of their supernatural revelation from God, we cannot enter into it except by a faint, recognitive stirring.

I wonder if you will feel that stirring as I tell you about a Tuesday morning that same fall at Regent when God made himself known to me even more unmistakably. Dr. Jim Houston came into my office, sat down, and said, almost without preamble, "I know that often in your life you have felt abandoned—by a father who was away preaching most of the time, by uncaring friends, now by Harold whose death has left you alone, and by God. I believe that you will only find an answer to your sense of abandonment in *self-abandonment*, in willingness to give away to God your self, your identity. You've been walking through a long, black tunnel. Soon you will see light ahead of you, and when you come out of the tunnel you'll find yourself on the edge of a cliff. *You must throw yourself off the cliff edge and trust that God will catch you in his arms.*" Startling words. They made me shiver because I had indeed felt the chill of that abandonment. But they also brought me the tingle of anticipation. I knew I needed to take this wise friend's words seriously; I needed to think through all the implications of his message from God to me, with its prophetic ring, so that I would know *how* to throw myself off the cliff.

The word Jim had used, "abandon," appealed to me. All my life I'd been urged by spiritual leaders to "yield," to "surrender" to God, to "relinquish" my idols. Through overuse those words had lost their impact and freshness for me, but the wildness, the impulsiveness of the word "abandon" challenged me to take this new risk.

On Tuesdays, people at Regent meet in small groups to pray and grow together in friendship. Journal in hand, I went to my car with Laurie, a young mother, her baby, and the baby's stroller, which I had to load into the trunk. We drove to the home where our group met, and when I got there I realized, with a sick jolt of panic, that the journal was gone.

Frantic, I rushed back to the campus in the car and checked in my office, then followed my cold trail through the building and out again to the parking lot. No journal. As I walked back to my car in the rain, I felt the interior tremor, the recognition of what this event really meant. My journal is an extension of me, as important as arm or leg. In it I feel my life condensed, myself embodied: my most personal observations and ideas and reflections are expressed and recorded in it in a way intensely valuable to me as a tracking of my life. I could buy another new, blank journal and start in again to reflect on its pages, but to lose this one, three-quarters full, was like losing myself. *Losing myself* . . . Suddenly I knew what was happening—God was pressing in for my gift. He was telling me the *how* of abandonment.

I gulped, then found myself saying, inwardly, This is

almost too painful to contemplate, but yes, if my journal stands for what you want from me, I'll give it up to you. I'll abandon it, and throw myself off the cliff edge. But oh, please be there to catch me!

Still shaking, I drove back to the prayer group. As I pushed open the front door, Laurie met me and said, beaming, "Karen Cooper just phoned to say she'd found your journal in a puddle in the middle of University Avenue. You can pick it up at her house this afternoon." I realized that as I drove away from Regent it must have fallen off the top of the car, where I'd put it while stowing the stroller in the trunk.

Later, when Karen, my student and friend, handed the soggy journal back to me, there was a tire print stippled across its familiar, ugly, orange front cover, its back cover was half ripped off, and the coiled binding of its spine was bent and flattened. But it had been given back to me. I had made the jump. God had made the catch.

Karen and I prayed our exhilaration and thanks. She wondered aloud to me: "And some people doubt the personal involvement of God in their lives? Why should I, who knew you so well, and knew where to call you, be the one to stop my car in the rain, to find out what it was that had caught my eye, lying in that puddle? Why did I stop at all? Traffic was heavy. There were scores of cars and bicycles and pedestrians traveling on that busy street. But I found the journal and saw your name written on the front."

In the same journal that night I wrote the story, and its conclusion:

> *If I am willing to abandon my will to God, broken like the spine of this journal, imprinted with God's own tire-track signature, he will give it back, and my identity*

with it. Oh, I feel it so profoundly, pierced to the core with its reality. God does care for me. He has not abandoned me. I have been "knocked breathless by his powerful glance." He showed himself, beaming his light to my heart in a true epiphany.

SHROVE TUESDAY

◆

Emilie Griffin

One of my earliest childhood memories is of rising early on Mardi Gras Day for the parade. I remember being dressed as a clown. Everything else is lit up by the radiance of early memory. Parents, grandparents, kitchen noises, cold weather, even the distant sound of drums and music, all these are engraved in my heart.

In stark contrast, I remember the twenty years I lived away from New Orleans and experienced Shrove Tuesday as most American Christians do. To most, the day is unknown, unheralded, except as perhaps an exotic festival that occurs elsewhere. In liturgical churches that commemorate the

Christian year, Shrove Tuesday is observed, but barely, rarely.

Masking is the central experience of the festival, though not everyone masks. But masking is a sign, I think, of surrendering completely to the exuberant spirit. Filtered through decades of memory, two different costumes that I wore stand out.

Once in college days a friend and I went as showboat minstrels in blackface. This was long ago, in a time when relations between blacks and whites were less politicized. Our gesture was greeted with amusement, not anger. My friend and I bought seersucker suits in a secondhand store on Rampart Street; we bought straw boater hats and decorated them with Mardi Gras ribbon, purple, green and gold. I realize now how much I wanted to celebrate the African-American culture of New Orleans, which is so much a part of the excitement of the holiday.

On another Mardi Gras, I was costumed as Joan of Arc. What gave me such an idea? No doubt on some level I was experiencing my own call to holiness. I was a senior in college, studying theater as well as literature, and under the influence of the French playwright Jean Anouilh and his American translator, Lillian Hellman. I had seen Hellman's translation of Anouilh's play *The Lark*, about the life of Joan of Arc, performed on Broadway the summer before. I had even (on behalf of *Mademoiselle* magazine) interviewed the producer, Kermit Bloomgarden. At the time I was strongly attracted by the theater. I was deeply affected by Julie Harris's performance as the Maid of Orleans. I recall the scene between Joan and the Bishop of Beauvais, played by Boris Karloff, the only time I ever saw him in a tender and fatherly role. Both their voices were remarkable, seizing the audience with great emotion and power. Unwittingly, I embraced my own future then and began to reflect on the power of plays to change our hearts.

I don't remember much about my day as Joan of Arc. The costume set me apart, revealed my high seriousness. (Most Mardi Gras costumes are funny.) I do remember dancing with a young man from another group. A friend of mine from childhood, he was a fine dancer and a good celebrator, in spite of a dark streak in his nature. He later wrote a one-of-a-kind novel that revealed a deep love of the distinctive folkways of New Orleans, *A Confederacy of Dunces*. The author, John Kennedy Toole, was dead by the time his book was published and acclaimed, but it did win a Pulitzer Prize.

Shrovetide, according to the *Oxford English Dictionary*, is three days: Sunday, Monday, and Tuesday, observed anciently as a time for confession before the forty-days-in-the-wilderness of Lent. In England, Shrove Tuesday is also called Pancake Day. In French countries and French Louisiana, Shrove Tuesday is Fat Tuesday, Mardi Gras.

For a long time now I have been conscious of a deep spiritual power in this festival. It is a spirituality of the marketplace, of the particular, of the here-and-now. This feast day is a sort of Punch-and-Judy show of the human spirit. And I can't help thinking that it fits with the example of our rabbi who ate and drank and made merry with his disciples. Like Christmas, it is a Christianizing of a pagan holiday; Mardi Gras is deeply connected to early earth- and folk-religion. This time of hilarity, like May Day or Midsummer's Eve, brings out the fool in us, the actor who sees life as a work of the imagination.

In New Orleans the festival has taken on very large proportions, beginning at Twelfth Night and offering a long season of merriment day and night: street parades with floats, trinkets being thrown to the crowds by masked revelers, marching bands, and formal balls with courts and pageantry. Liturgically, this celebration is like Hallowe'en, the shadow side of a great opportunity for holiness. But the spirit of rejoicing in this feast is more like a second Christmas, a time for the people, the working classes, to be temporarily set free from cares and obligations. It is a release from the bondage of winter (which though not always cold, can be very rainy and bitter in New Orleans) and a time to cherish friendship and simplicity of heart.

The chief attitude of the holiday is one of peaceful revolution. When the spirit rules, the kingdoms of this world are overturned. For one day of the year, the Mayor of New Orleans issues a proclamation. He surrenders the controls of government to Rex, a make-believe Mardi Gras king. Rex and his dukes and knights are mock-nobility, whose code of honor is one of hilarity and foolishness. Their motto is *pro bono publico*, for the good of the people. This spirit in some ways makes concrete the words of Mary's canticle:

Thou hast put down the mighty from their thrones, and exalted them of low degree.

The capacity for make-believe is part of our childlikeness. It is this talent we may exercise (not often enough) when we pray and when we play. To make believe is to express a hope that things may be more perfect, happier, more glorious, more heavenly, more humorous. Mardi Gras is a moment when we may (if we enter into it fully) remember and act out again our heart's desire.

The colors of Mardi Gras in New Orleans are purple, green and gold. These are the colors of chivalry and kingship. A mighty imagery is threaded through the festival, and the power of music and dance creates a liturgy of joy, a spectacle of spontaneity and imagination.

The clubs that celebrate on the days between Twelfth Night (Epiphany) and Ash Wednesday (the beginning of Lent) are known in New Orleans as "mystick krewes." I think that is a clue to the mystical nature of this unruly holiday.

The song adopted by Rex as the Mardi Gras theme song in 1872 was first performed in the burlesque known as "Blue Beard" during the visit of the Grand Duke Alexis. This became part of the Rex tradition, and for me the song, with its passion, humor and hilarity, has come to mean something about the intimacy between God and the soul:

If ever I cease to love
If ever I cease to love
May the moon be turned into green cheese
If ever I cease to love.

In my book *Chasing the Kingdom*, which used fairy-tale materials and children's books to create a new parable of the spiritual journey, I wrote a Cinderella story in which my character is invited to a royal ball in Mousedom and is whirled into a passionate waltz by the Mystick King of Mouse. The literary roots of this, I later saw, were in Hans Christian Andersen as well as the Brothers Grimm. Fairy tales celebrate not only the joy but the inner darkness of the human spirit. Masquerade makes it possible to tell the awful secrets that lie buried deep within us and through the blessing of laughter to understand that, in the end, the deep sins of the human heart are forgiven and there is nothing to be afraid of.

The street festivals of New Orleans Mardi Gras are raucous, sometimes even dangerous, and this has been true from the first such event in 1840. It is no accident that the first Mardi Gras krewe was called Comus, and this was a revisiting of Milton's *Comus*, in which a wicked spirit attempts to lead a virtuous young woman astray. New Orleans law requires even today that the masks must be taken off at sundown, even though the festival continues until midnight.

Today I celebrate Mardi Gras very quietly, usually in my mother's company, remembering and reflecting upon the meaning of the holiday. For us it is possible to cherish the past, to love, especially, the tradition of music and masquerade, and to hope that the high poetry and symbolic beauty of this feast, which is of the people, by the people and for the people, will not perish from the earth.

In a time when my city and country are gripped by a crisis of literacy, I am conscious of the strong literary tradition that is present here. Most of the parades are built on literary themes—themes from the great books, sagas from Homer, Vergil, heroics from Shakespeare, Chaucer, Beowulf. As yet the influence of films and television is not pervasive. It seems as if an older, classical and high literary culture is being preserved here.

Again, the motif of nobility is strong. The nobility is not of an established class culture but rather the nobility of the human spirit. Though many Mardi Gras organizations are exclusive, nevertheless the spirit of the festival is egalitarian, celebrating the kingship of everyman.

The interweaving of Christian meaning and pagan mythology is one of the most striking features of Mardi Gras. The parades, with their high mythological quality, seem to me to be almost a recollection of earlier centuries in literature, the times of Shakespeare and Milton. I remember vividly seeing giant papier-mâché heads of Shakespeare and Dante on floats as they pass, and remember that the creative spirit is so often celebrated in Mardi Gras mythmaking.

And another incident comes to mind, a reunion with one of my teachers, Dr. Mildred Christian, on Mardi Gras Day, 1985. An internationally known scholar, Miss Christian was one of three teachers who had powerfully schooled me in English literature and helped me to grasp the poetic spirit as a sign of God's presence in us.

Then retired from Newcomb College, where she taught for forty years, Miss Christian had given up her New Orleans house and had gone to live at St. Anna's residence, not far from the main parade route. The streets were filled with maskers and revelers. Together we walked two blocks to stand in the chill wind and wait for the parade of Rex, king of this unruly festival, to pass by. A young man suddenly approached us with a bunch of long-stemmed yellow chrysanthemums and pressed them into Miss Christian's hands. I understood his sudden affectionate impulse. Miss Christian's shining face was an invitation to friendship. Later, after leaving her, I walked on the grounds of my high school, meditating on how God had constantly broken through to me through books, through teachers, through poetry. From the upstairs balcony of the school, I had a partial view of the parade, and one word, only one, on the side of a passing truck-float, stayed in view for a long moment. The word was HEAVEN.

My presumption, as a believer, is that no event is entirely

secular. The word *holy* is hidden inside the word *holiday*. In every commemoration, whether of some moment in our collective history as a nation or a greeting-card occasion such as mother's day or father's day, the spirit of the One God can be spied when one looks with eyes of faith.

Mardi Gras is seen by theologians as an event in which sacred and secular have a direct encounter, a clash, even a collision. Nathan A. Scott, Jr., in a theological reflection entitled "The House of Intellect in an Age of Carnival," alludes to the literary theory of Mikhail Bakhtin, who makes Carnival fundamental to his theory of the novel. (See *The Whirlwind in Culture: Frontiers in Theology*, in honor of Langdon Gilkey, Meyer Stone Books, 1988.)

"For Bakhtin," Scott says, "a time of carnival is one in which 'life [is] drawn out of the usual rut' or is in some radical way 'turned inside out.' . . . Things that are normally separate and distinct are brought together, so that 'the sacred combines with the profane, the lofty with the low, the great with the insignificant, the wise with the stupid.' " Scott sees, following Bakhtin, that Carnival is a metaphor for openness to contradictions, to uncertainty and darkness, that characterizes the literary imagination. His principal argument is that our culture is dominated by pluralism ("the game we are fated to play"). But this, he says, means "we must seek to win that special virtue which will enable us to dwell amid uncertainty and ambiguity and contrariety—and this, of course, is the virtue that Keats speaks of as Negative Capability."

Scott mentions Carnival as a reference point for the disunity of our culture and the artist's need to tolerate this diversity. For him, the inner symbolism of Mardi Gras is that the master-slave relationship is (for one day at least) set aside, making way for openness and dialogue.

Another theological commentator on Mardi Gras, from quite a different and unexpected quarter, is Joseph Cardinal Ratzinger, who is seen today as a sharply conservative voice, one who constantly returns to long-held Christian belief and tradition. For him, Mardi Gras—in German, *Fasching*—is "certainly not a Church festival" but at the same time "unthinkable" apart from the Christian year. In his small work of reflections, *Seek That Which Is Above* (San Francisco: Ignatius Press, 1986) Ratzinger sees this festival as part of the narrative of Christian stories celebrating the rhythm of the earth. Especially does he take note of its roots in the Feast of Purim in the Jewish calendar, "which recalls the deliverance of the Jews from the menace of persecution."

As I read Ratzinger's words I suddenly remember looking down from my upstairs bedroom window on a wintry New York day and seeing the figure of a child in a formal coat and dress shoes, wearing a large papier-mâché head. She was representing Queen Esther, and she went from house to house in this residential New York neighborhood, bringing gifts to her neighbors, who represented "the poor."

"The joyful abandon," Ratzinger goes on, "with which this feast is celebrated is intended to express the feeling of liberation, and on this day it is not only a memory but a promise: the person who is in the hands of the God of Israel is already, in anticipation, freed from the snares of his enemies."

How remarkable, I think, that Ratzinger should know! Out of his German childhood, perhaps, and his world-knowledge of the Christian experience, he accepts the abandon of Mardi Gras as a sign of spiritual freedom.

But what will he say of the traces of paganism that remain in this feast, of the kingship of Bacchus and Comus and Momus and Proteus and Hermes?

Christians, he says, no longer have anything to fear from the demons. The true God has triumphed over these. The life-and-death struggle with the demons becomes an occasion for laughter before the seriousness of Lent. The masquerade shows us what we also see in the Psalms and the Prophets: the freedom of the One God in contrast to those who still serve many gods.

In February 1991 I spent Purim in New York with Jewish friends on that remarkable day which was also seen as the end of the Gulf War. Representing Queen Esther, a young man came to the house with a candy effigy of Uncle Sam. Somehow, for me, this patriotic icon became a Mardi Gras metaphor, celebrating the liberated heart.

ASH WEDNESDAY

Robert Siegel

Blackbird in the Chimney

We hear his feet scrabble against the sheet metal,
Trying for an impossible foothold. The frantic wings
Beat and beat helplessly in the liner pipe
That tapers toward the top. What intricate
Dark way did he find down into this crevice
Looking for a likely place to nest? Some strange

Instinct led him under the metal collar
Around the chimney top where his kind pause
To chatter briefly every spring—before heading on

Like punctuation scattered to the clouds
Floating in a long sentence across March.
He's trapped for sure. Sometimes one or two

Will fluster down the main pipe. At the bottom
When the damper opens, the disheveled pair
Will squawk and flap wildly into the light,
True to the old saw, *The way up is down.*
Luckily, their small hell has a convenient exit.
But his is sealed—the only way out is up.

I unscrew the metal chimney top and search
With a flashlight a crevice twenty feet deep.
The pipe curves: I cannot see the bottom.
Meanwhile his every feather and claw's slightest
Twitch is magnified by the metal liner.
"He's here. He's right here. I can hear him—"

My daughter's voice comes up from the fireplace,
Shaking at his proximity, delicate as his bones.
"It's only a bird," I call down to her. "It doesn't
    suffer—
Not the way we would suffer. A bird can't think
That it *has* suffered—*is* suffering—*will* suffer."
So ends my conjugation, muffled in the pipe.

"Still—he suffers," she says, and for a moment
The bird is still. Then the scrabbling resumes.
I lower a triple hook on fishing line
Again and again. No luck. But my doing something
Helps her and helps me too on that windy roof,
One step from rotten gutters. Once, I see the gleam

Of an eye and imagine I've caught him. For two days
I climb up and down the ladder with ever more
Elaborate schemes until the scratching stops
And reluctantly I tell her nothing will work.
"Two days"—the Humane Society says on the
      phone—
"A third and, believe us, it's finished for sure."

My daughter is growing up. She understands.
She doesn't want her father to take more risks.
Her silence matches mine now, holding, as it does,
The neighbor drowned in a river, the classmate dying
Of leukemia, the jogger struck down quadraplegic.
Her dad couldn't help this time, unlike the time

He drilled through the kitchen wall at 1 A.M.
Behind the refrigerator to make an exit
For the shy and unwilling-to-be-rescued
Hamster, who finally came out for cheese
And her maternal wheedling. Or the time
He released the gerbil from the cooled-off furnace

After listening for his scratching on the pipes.
That one died of old age in his sleep,
A seer, having passed on (if gerbils can)
A vision to his cagemate of a cold
Dark place at the bottom, an impenetrable wall,
Hunger, thirst, and fear—when suddenly,
Beyond all expectation, the wall opened
And light came through and a warm human hand.

ANNUNCIATION

❦

Walter Wangerin, Jr.

The annunciation by the angel Gabriel to the virgin Mary that she would conceive in her womb a child, a son, whom she should call "Jesus," must be recognized as a singular event and altogether unique. It happened once. It will never happen again. There was but one Christ, one such holy and virginal birth, one Son of God only. Gabriel could not have made the same announcement twice.

But I wish he would.

Once only did Jesus gather flesh in a human womb, bone and brain and mild eyes and hands so small, so small, that the spikes one day to pierce them were thicker than they and longer than his little arms. Brutal metal, banged into shape by hammers on harder anvils—the spikes in those baby days were far away. This infant was a tissue knit in love in Mary's deepest, sweetest interior. This baby grew in a warm sea, in Mary's amnion, under Mary's gentle attention, under Mary's two hands as she felt the roll of his heel across the equator of her waist and she smiled and she closed her eyes and she loved him.

All this but once.

Therefore, Gabriel's particular prophecy of the Holy Spirit's "coming upon" such a one as this, his prophecy that "the power of the Most High will overshadow" her, and then the woman's own most humble response, "Let it be to me according to your word," all can have occurred but one time too.

But I genuinely wish that it might be again.

And that I might be that woman.

I beg a bright annunciation of angels!

I plead an indwelling of the Christ—in me, in this particular body and spirit, this standing, breathing dust, this Walter Wangerin, Jr.

I, too, would bow and in perfect submission would murmur, "Unto me, unto me according to your word." With God shall nothing be impossible? Then I beseech the Deity for a pregnancy of my own.

This, as close as one may know so private a moment, is what happened:

A young woman is attending to some common thing in solitude, her head bowed down to her labor, intent, alone, but in no wise lonely. Is she patting dough? Praying? Sewing? Marking the ground in the courtyard with her index finger, meditating?

Perhaps her hair is undone and hanging like a veil around her head, and in her hand a comb, and in her mind glad, wandering thoughts of the future: she is betrothed. She soon shall marry. The man's name is Joseph, a just man by public reputation, a kind man in her own experience, a man obedient to promptings of the Lord. Well, and if she is indeed lost in such ponderings, then she is happy. An uncomplicated life, a calm and predictable future.

Look: just at the corner of her mouth a small smile curls.

But suddenly light streaks the air around her. Dazzling, perfectly silent flashes of lightning strike all in one place, causing the face of a glorious being now beaming down on her—and his raiment is whiter than snow.

Bathed in radiance, here is . . . (there is no doubt of this, though one may never have met such another messenger, may never have seen these supernal powers of the Almighty) . . . an angel!

The angel Gabriel has come from God to a city in Galilee named Nazareth, to a virgin in that city: Mary.

And Mary can scarcely look at him, for he is one who stands in the presence of God. But Mary looks at him nonetheless, because her nature, however obedient, is straightforward.

Mary has a boldness.

The angel speaks: "Hail, O favored one! The Lord is with you."

Favored? Mary thinks, startled. *Favored? Favored? What does that mean?* Who is she that the Lord should look at her?

She frowns and bites her bottom lip.

Gabriel makes an immediate rustling sound, as though he were solid and moved his arms and the luminous fabric brushed itself. He raises his hands, gesturing comfort: "Don't be afraid," he says. He calls her by name: "Mary," he whispers, "you've found favor with God. You have nothing to fear."

An angel of consolations! Concerned for her peace, even now! Come to declare God's wonderful plan to take people from darkness to marvelous light, yet Gabriel pauses to ease the maiden!

And she is eased. She is not greatly afraid. But neither does she rise or in any way move. She waits.

And the angel says in an intimate voice, like an aunt or a cousin, "Listen: you're going to conceive in your womb and bear a son, and when you do you must name him Jesus."

Something in Mary contracts to hear this. Her eyes and her mouth draw tight, but her gaze remains steadfastly in the light. She watches the flaming face of Gabriel, even as that light intensifies, even as the angel's voice grows formal before her, ascending to the sing-song rhythms of grand proclamations:

> *"He will be great!*
>> *He will be known as the son of the Highest!*
> *The Lord God will give him*
>> *The throne of his father, King David, forever!*
> *And the king and the kingdom,*
>> *This Lord over Jacob,*
>>> *Will reign in the world without end."*

Now Mary, still not dropping her eyes from the angel, moves. She straightens up on her knees and lifts a finger and signals a question.

The message of the messenger of the almighty God is interrupted, and Gabriel is forced to stop his song.

Mary is not embarrassed. She's bold. Moreover, she's got common sense. "Excuse me," she says, "but how can this happen when I have never known a man?"

A problem. Perhaps heavenly beings don't understand the ways of earthly bodies and require the instruction of sensible maidens. Mary would be willing to explain.

On the other hand, regarding the heart of the virgin herself, perhaps the promise is of such glory that nothing, absolutely nothing, should hinder it for her, and every problem ought to be solved that the path be never so smooth: *A baby? A baby for Mary? A son, the Messiah? O God my Savior, let it be—but how can it be? How could such a thing happen?*

Is it now that the woman's face takes something of the angel's fire? Is it now she begins to blush?

Excitement under stern restraint: "Sir, how can this be—?"

And the angel answers again in a song, singing of the divine conceiving. Gabriel fills the place where Mary is. His light allows no shadow of turning, no dimness in the Lord's ability to do as he promised to do:

"The Holy Spirit will come on you,
The power of God o'ershadow you,
So the baby to be born of you,
    Will be holy indeed—
    The Son of God!"

Now the angel softens the clustered lightning and his eyes. He mutes his voice and matches sense for sense with Mary. He speaks of this uncommon thing, now, in common language, on the level of a common woman whose concerns are realistic as well as divine.

"Listen, Mary," he says, for all the world like an aunt or a cousin, "even old Elizabeth, your relative, has conceived a son. This is her sixth month, although she was barren. Do you see? No saying of God shall ever be impossible."

Yes, the fire is surely in the face of Mary now. Her eyes dance. They dart a joyful flame, even as she bows her head in faithful compliance. *A baby! A baby!*

"Behold," the virgin murmurs, "I am the handmaid of the Lord." She is dignified and grave and beautiful in her obedience. But she is also a young woman trembling with the sweetness of the thing: *Mary's going to have a baby! God has regarded her low estate! Everyone shall call her blessed! A baby!*

"Let it happen to me," she whispers, wishing the wish herself since God's command and her desire are one and the same, "let it happen to me according to your word."

So the bright light vanishes. So the angel withdraws and leaves her there.

So Mary . . . what? Mary does what now? Covers her burning face a moment to think of this thing? Raises her flashing eyes, peering here and there at common things and seeing nothing common at all, but the glory of heaven around her? Mary does what? Stands up? Lifts her arms? Bursts into laughter and twirls herself about in ineffable joy?

A baby! My spirit rejoices in God my Savior—a baby boy, Messiah, Son of God!

"Listen! Listen! Somebody has to hear this thing! I'm going to have a baby!"

I think, before she raced to Elizabeth to combine their blessings in companionship, I think that Mary wept and laughed together. I think she repeated the promise over and over, not in doubt, for the angel had spoken it after all, but in wonder.

In utter trust and confidence: " 'You will conceive in your womb and bear a son.' Oh, my! Oh, my! He who is mighty has done great things for me, and holy is his name!"

Thus the event of the Annunciation, which the church has remembered by a special feast day ever since the sixth century. The festival originated in Constantinople. Throughout the ages common folk have called it "Lady Day"—and always it has been observed on March 25, exactly nine months before Christmas. So the church considered these two times, that of Gabriel's announcement and that of Mary's conceiving, not to be too far from each other.

As the angel declared it, so it was, so quickly thereafter.

Mary heard and saw and believed and agreed and got pregnant.

And then the dear Lord Jesus was gathering flesh within her.

And all this happened but once for all.

I wish it could happen again.

Our assignment throughout this volume has been to find the personal experience correlative with the holy day before us. How has this particular celebration of the church year *felt* to us? Or, if our own denomination hasn't celebrated the festival, then what personal remembrance gives feeling and reality to the Biblical event that it commemorates?

Christmas, of course, is easy. Everyone has had some experience both with the religious celebration and with the event of Jesus' birth. Who would not have a story to tell in relationship with that day?

But the Annunciation, nine months prior, in one whose tradition (Lutheran) did not regularly observe the Annunciation, is not so easy.

My own childhood remembers nothing of the day.

My Biblical reading does. The story itself is wonderfully familiar. It seemed to me, therefore, that I would have little trouble in calling forth the personal experience *like unto* this event: Mary, confronted by the angel Gabriel, hearing in her own ears the promise of the Christ within her.

But nothing in my life is like this. Not anything.

The experience that sincerely arises in me as I contemplate the appearance of angels, then, is an immediate one. One present, but presently incomplete. It is happening now, even as I write, here in my soul: it is a desiring.

I yearn for the bright, convincing, palpable appearing of the angels before me! *Dear Lord, I wish I could see your messengers, your burning, spiritual ministers of power and goodness, them that stand in your presence before they descend to ours.*

But I don't.

I believe in the existence of the angels. I do not doubt that they are. They are. Gabriel, "Hero of God," first came to Daniel in a vision as a man, revealing what was to come in the Day of Judgment (how privy, then, to the mind of God!), interpreting visions, granting understanding and wisdom (how close, then, to the human mind!).

Hosts of angels and various orders of angels attend the mighty God. So John the Divine was shown in his Revelation, where the seven spirits (archangels?) are the means of critical messages to seven churches, where four holy creatures wait upon the throne of God, where four great angels preside at the four corners of the earth, powers of the universe—and besides these there are myriads of myriads and thousands of thousands praising the Lamb who is worthy to receive power: angels!

And the Apostle Paul again and again refers to the "powers," angels who, if not always congenial with God, are yet beneath his governance. There are, too, the overtly rebellious angels "who did not keep their own position but left their proper dwelling." These, says Jude, "have been kept by him in eternal chains in the nether gloom until the judgment of the great day." I do not understand this, but I believe it.

I believe in the complex, busy life of a spiritual world, both good and evil, of God or else against God. I do not pretend I could describe it, nor do I swallow wholesale the descriptions of credulous people, kindly people, pious people, to be sure, but people imbued with something besides the sharp restrictions and careful promptings of Holy Scripture and its proper interpretation. I recognize how much folklore must have distorted it, how transcendent, in fact, this angelic community is, how inaccessible to my created, prosaic mind. I cannot, by my own reason, strength, art, or piety, rise to it.

But I believe in it!

And I maintain a healthy fear regarding it, as well as an almost inexpressible fondness. I am glad that there are angels! I move, I know, in a vast company of bodiless beings, as one who walks among geese on an Alaskan shoreline. Almost, I can hear the whirr of the wings, the multitudinous alleluias, the hosts declaring, *Gloria in excelsis Deo!*

Almost. Not quite.

In my fleshly ear there sits the silence of the mortal world, the creation severed by sin from God, into which the Christ was mortally born to save it after all.

Well, but when that silence grows occlusive, grieving me; when I feel most childlike, small and weak and lonely;

when flesh itself insists on attention, and I feel less and less a spiritual being (though I am!), more and more the mortal one—*Lord, then I wish I could hear the angels.*

Is it faithlessness to desire Mary's experience? No, I don't think so. Is it arrogance? No. Mary's position is one of perfect humility. What then? Well, weariness. A sense of the loss of the resource of self. Like Elijah, traveling from danger to Mount Horeb and falling asleep beneath his broom tree, it is the exhaustion of this flesh, the fatigue of the created.

An angel restored that prophet with a touch and a cake and a jar of water—twice. And in the strength of that food, Elijah went forty days and forty nights to Horeb, the mount of God.

Holy God, please do not blame me. Hear me. Comfort me. Precisely because the times have progressed by science and technologies to knowledge and control of your natural universe; precisely because the people are proud in the imagination of their own hearts, scorning your name and matters spiritual; because the mighty still hold their thrones, and the low are low, and the hungry are hungry still—please help your servant.

Lift me by an angel's touch and a little food.

Allow me, sometime, the light of the archangel—not that I be snatched from this existence, but that I might the more strongly abide herein, assured of the growth of the Christ within me.

O let this heavy flesh be granted, yet in the flesh, a little light. Gabriel's effulgence.

Like the angel who sat on the stone when Jesus had arisen.

My Lord, I beg an annunciation of angels.

Again, again—

Amen.

LENT

❦

John Leax

I keep this journal in the seclu-
sion of my cabin on Remnant Acres, my five-acre woodlot
across the Genesee Valley from one of New York State's
potential radioactive waste dumps. I named these acres to
stand for my commitment to live within the bounds of nature's limits and the terms of stewardship imposed on me by
Scripture. I write on the backs of old manuscripts and hand-
outs from class. I have enough to last me years, yet each day
I make more. I make so many that one day last summer I
filled a stump hole with papers, committed them to the soil,
to become soil, and covered them with earth.

Today it is bitter cold on Remnant Acres. The temperature is not so low, but a hard wind sweeps across the field from the northwest and swirls the snow into drifts. Because I have been away, the cabin has been unattended for a week. When I came in carrying my little propane heater, I saw the thin film of ice that forms in the low spot on my writing table was larger than usual, and I could not begin to write until I thawed it and wiped it up with a towel I keep for just that purpose.

The regular appearance of that sheet of ice (or on warm days puddle of water) disturbs me, for I cannot find its source. To all appearances my cabin is tight. I've caulked every crack I can find at least twice. Still the water, insistent and insidious, finds its way in and waits in the center of my table to disrupt my work. What is maddening is that the trail that should allow me to follow the water to the leak has always evaporated.

Today as I waited for it to melt, I saw it as an analogy for the way sin, as subtle as water, finds the hidden cracks in my life, flows to the center of my work, and disrupts the wholeness of all my relationships. That is a good analogy to consider on Ash Wednesday, for an awareness of sin and a determination to be cleansed is the order of this day. But since the passing of my adolescence, I have never been able to focus long on my evil nature, nor on any particular acts of either omission or commission. I live rather in the awareness of my redemption, of the work of restoration Christ is doing in me and in creation.

Almost as soon as I drew the analogy of sin infiltrating like water, my imagination leaped ahead to another: Christ the living water infiltrating, coming on his own even when we are unaware, uninviting, to bring life to the land. These woods I love are filled with springs. In a few weeks the thaw will come and I will walk nowhere in them apart from water.

MARCH 1

Eight below this morning. When I came into the cabin, my chair was frozen to the floor where the snow had melted from my boots yesterday. To keep warm I have my heater under my table. My legs feel as if I'm standing over a fire, but the rest of me is just about comfortable. That probably has something to do with the extra down vest I have on under my sweatshirt. As I sat here thinking about the day, I saw a bit of yellow protruding from a hole in my pocket. Naturally I pulled on it and drew an 18-inch strip of ribbon out, an ACNAG support ribbon.

Allegany County Non-violent Action Group is just one of the groups organized to oppose the siting of a nuclear waste dump in this the poorest, least populated county in New York. It is the group that, after a long struggle, I have chosen to become a part of. Ten months ago when the group formed, I thought it wrongheaded, or at least wrong for me. I thought then that the mounting of scientific evidence (trust in experts) and appeals to the judicial system (belief in good intentions and justice) were appropriate. What I have seen since then has changed my mind. Scientific evidence has been ignored or explained away.

Three times now, since December, by using roadblocks and accepting arrests, members of ACNAG have denied the siting commission access to the proposed Allegany County sites for "walk-overs." Each time I have participated and have worn a yellow support ribbon. I have carried coffee, coordinated communications, and have worked the crowd helping to keep the nonviolent commitment firm. About forty people have been arrested. Most have pleaded guilty to disturbing the peace and have been fined $5.00 plus court costs.

Last week, however, a New York State Supreme Court justice in Buffalo issued a blanket injunction against anyone interfering with the siting process. The cost of defending the earth has suddenly risen. Defenders now face contempt of court charges, fines up to $1000, and thirty-day jail sentences.

For years I have been writing about the earth, about the Christian responsibility to hold the earth against Christ's coming, to offer it up to him whole, productive, and healthy. This injunction has forced me to rethink my involvement. Integrity demands that I stand behind my words and bear the cost of my commitment. I am now wearing the orange ribbon of one willing to go to jail.

MARCH 2

None of this is a great adventure. I want only to come to husband this small portion of earth given over to my stewardship.

My thoughts turn to this season; I see Christ in the garden. His perfect imagination must have felt every pain in advance. He asked for the cup to be removed. Then he said "Yes" to what he knew was coming. He said "Yes" before he knew if he had the strength to bear the consequences of it.

I also see Peter beside the fire, challenged to identify himself with Christ. And I see him fail. I taste in my mouth his words, "I do not know him." And I feel rising in me the desire to say, "I don't have to do this."

And I pray for the cup to be removed.

MARCH 6

This morning, as I sit here in the quiet, I am conscious that I live not only in this world but in Christ. In this world I act out the terms of my salvation with fear and trembling. But it is Christ working in me that sanctifies my actions. And that changes everything. It does not mean that the dump does not matter. It means, rather, I have nothing to do but be faithful, to offer myself, prepared for whatever Christ desires. To place my body on the arrest line, to write these words. To withdraw, to be silent. To discern the moment when it comes. To refuse to worry until then.

MARCH 9

I think of myself as a man without enemies. To the extent that I am Christ's man in this world, however, I must admit that the enemies of Christ are my enemies. And I must learn to name them enemies.

Eugene Peterson talks about hate in the context of holiness in the Psalms. He writes, ". . . we see clearly what we never saw before, the utter and terrible sacrilege of enemies who violate a good creation, who brutalize women and men who are made, everyone of them, in the image of God. There is an enormous amount of suffering epidemic in the world because of evil people. The rape and pillage are so well concealed in polite language and courteous conventions that some people can go years without seeing it. And we ourselves did not see it."

Too often I confuse holy with nice, and choose niceness. I lack the passionate rage of an Amos or a Hosea.

Well, I can no longer praise tolerance. I have enemies: men who rape children, corporations who elevate profit over health, advertisers who sell their cheap goods, people who drive drunk, teachers who lie, abortionists who make no distinctions, right-to-lifers who have no compassion, food processors and grocery chains that have destroyed the health of a people, agri-business men who have destroyed the health of the soil. The nuclear industry that destroys the earth for its stockholders, politicians who protect the wealthy from the health hazards of the nuclear industry but who will not lift a finger to protect the poor and powerless from the same hazards, and judges who turn the judicial system into an instrument of oppression.

MARCH 10

Today I found the leak in my cabin. It rained as I worked; a tiny trickle of water flowed across the table. I knelt down and looked up under a small ledge and discovered a nail acting as a wick. How efficiently it works!

SECOND SUNDAY IN LENT

We had in church, this morning, a time of intercessory prayer. Knowing that I and the other members of ACNAG will confront the siting commission and violate the injunction when it attempts a "walk-over" on Thursday, I went to the altar. Were it not for the weeks of prayer and fasting engaged in by the church last fall as we considered our responses to the nuclear dump, I do not believe I could have made the decision I have made. As I knelt, I imagined the faces of as many resisters as I could call up and held them before God. I prayed for their safety, for their faithfulness and for their resources to maintain the nonviolent commitment. I prayed also for the police who will be called upon to enforce the injunction. Then I ceased to make petitions.

The sound of the organ worked slowly into my consciousness. The words that came to me were, ". . . and the things of the earth will grow strangely dim in the light of his glory and grace." What irony! Oh, I know the intent of the words, but I know also their falseness, the abuse they have permitted, and the opprobrium they have brought on the church. Words count. We dare not sing less than the whole truth. In the light of the glory and grace of Christ, the things of this world do not grow dim; they are transfigured; they are filled with glory and grace. And so are we.

MARCH 14

One day recently I compared the upcoming civil disobedience action to the cup Jesus prayed to have removed in the garden. For the moment it seems to have been removed. Sunday, at the ACNAG steering committee meeting, I learned that the commission planned to make its assault on the West Almond site. Because my duties as a monitor require me to stay at the Caneadea site no matter where the action occurs, I felt relief.

Still I faced the action scheduled for tomorrow with much anxiety. Then last evening I received a call; the commission had canceled its "walk-over." This morning as I drove I listened to the news and was startled to hear Angelo Orazzio, the commission chairman, quoted as saying the commission

would not come because a small group was threatening violence. There is no such group. His statement is designed to
gain public sympathy, to paint his opposition black, to por-
tray himself as an innocent public servant struggling to do
his duty. I'm angry and I'm finding it increasingly difficult
to hate the sin and love the sinner. At what point does a sinner
become his sin? At what point does the distinction cease to
matter? How am I to be a peacemaker when every day my
anger grows and my ability to moderate my emotions de-
creases? How am I to deal with the nightmares that come to
me when I sleep? What do I do with that streak in me that
finds it hard to care about the safety of the commission?

MARCH 15

I'm still thinking about enemies. Yesterday I got a letter from
John Bennett. In it he wrote, ". . . perhaps you can't write
satire because you have not yet become angry enough. Hate
the sin and love the sinner? I can't do that: a grave weakness
in my Christian being-ness, I suppose."

I wonder, is tolerance a characteristic of the young? Does
the ability to hate come with age? Strange phrasing for a
Christian—the ability to hate. Strange thoughts for Lent. I
should be confessing my hate and asking forgiveness, and
here I am meditating on it, nurturing it. I read in Psalm 5
yesterday morning,

> *For thou art not a God that hath pleasure in wickedness;*
> *neither shall evil dwell with thee.*
> *The foolish shall not stand in thy sight;*
> *thou hatest all workers of iniquity.*

Thou shalt destroy them that speak lies; . . .
Destroy thou them, O God;
let them fall by their own counsels . . .

The psalmist seems to make no distinctions between sinner and sin. Perhaps in practice we are our actions, we are our sins incarnated. Apart from me, my sins would not exist. By myself I am sin to the world. Redeemed, I am somehow made Christ to the world. Paul, I think, spoke of Christ becoming sin for our sakes.

THIRD SUNDAY IN LENT

Mike preached from Colossians this morning. His theme was the necessity of sacrifice to validate one's witness. He kept returning to Paul's imprisonment, the idea that it was the result and the proof of his faithfulness.

Every time he returned to it, I returned to Allegany County and the nuclear dump resistance. I have not yet been arrested. Indeed, since the January actions, no one has been arrested, for the authorities have acted to avoid confrontation. The last week has been entirely peaceful. And mostly I have directed my thoughts to other matters. But I have still been thinking of sacrifice. I have been thinking of my writing, of the work I do here each morning typing these pages. How do I offer up this work as a sacrifice to God? What cost will I be required to pay? What cost will this community be required to pay to validate its witness?

MARCH 19

My schedule today is disrupted by other duties. So I arrived anxious and annoyed. Cold has returned, and here on the hill, snow is slowly covering the woods' floor.

I set my heater under the desk and read psalms out loud until the table ice melted and I regained some equilibrium. In my anger at circumstances this morning, I read

> *O Lord my God, if I have done this;*
>   *if there be iniquity in my hands;*
> *if I have rewarded evil unto him that was at peace with*
>   *me . . .*
> *Let the enemy persecute my soul, and take it.*

When I began this journal, I said something about not being able to focus long on my sins, about moving directly to grace and being overwhelmed by it and by the restoration taking place. It seems, however, as I've meditated here, I've turned more and more to a consciousness of my own sinfulness. What I wonder this morning is, where will that take me? How will it lead me to change my life? My anger does not rise from jealousy or ambition. It rises out of a concern for the good then forgets to contain the good of all in its drive for the immediate good of a few. I'm too small. If I had the emotional range to empathize more broadly, perhaps I could comprehend the needs that drive others, the needs that make them act unjustly. Then I could act redemptively rather than vindictively.

MARCH 21

Since Sunday there have been rumors of changes in the low-level-nuclear-waste siting process. Members of the legislature have been meeting with Governor Cuomo. Yesterday a report on the noon news stated that the process was going to be halted, and I, along with some others, had a few hours of euphoria. The evening news, however, dashed all hope. What the governor proposed was to have the siting commissioner decide on a method of disposal (something they have claimed to be unable to do without a site) and then return to naming a site at a later date. The genius of his scheme is that while it gives the appearance of being responsive to the people, it allows the same forces presently in the public eye to continue their plot against the earth in private.

The absolute sinfulness of the process overwhelms me. I want to cry with the Psalmist, "Thou shalt destroy them that speak lies; the Lord will abhor the bloody and deceitful man."

MARCH 23

I dreamed last night that a great controversy raged in Houghton. Toys Я Us had purchased a plot of land near the college maintenance center and planned to build a large warehouse and distribution center. The community was divided over the project. Some were angry that the building would disturb the pastoral view and atmosphere. Others were furious at the implied insult to an academic community; toys and a backwards R!

How I wish that were the issue.

FOURTH SUNDAY IN LENT

I am upset about a conversation I had with a friend who supports the nuclear industry. I couldn't yesterday, and I still can't today, sort out how to balance friendship with opposition. It's easy to call the siting commission to judgment. It's difficult to do the same for a friend.

What is friendship worth? How much truth does one sacrifice? What is the cost of peace in our time?

The fourth Sunday in Lent is the halfway point. In his sermon this morning, Mike pointed out that traditionally this Sunday is a feast day, a hold in the process of introspection and focus on repentance to remember redemption, to remember Christ and to give thanks. It is a day of celebration.

We celebrated communion.

MARCH 28

I just finished reading Will Campbell's *Brother to a Dragonfly*. Because ACNAG is engaged in civil disobedience, our resistance is often compared to the civil rights movement. It is not an apt comparison; the differences between the two movements are greater than the likenesses. We personally risk much less than the civil rights workers, for we have the support of the community in which the action takes place, and we have at least a measure of sympathy from the police officers sent to deal with us.

The likeness exists in the resistance to injustice and oppression. Only to the extent that one is able to imagine the

creation a minority (one disenfranchised to be used) are we
part of the civil rights movement.

In all this I struggle with how I love the land because it
is the creation of the Lord, and how I also love those who
abuse it. I am called to do both. Individuals and the creation
cry out for redemption. As the messenger of the Good News,
I must articulate the full vision. If all I had to struggle with
were the officers of the siting commission, the politicians,
and the representatives of the growth-for-growth's-sake in-
dustries, I could simply call down fire. I could claim love
requires judgment. But that way masks anger. All I have
written about holy hatred leaves me unconvinced. It may be
true in the abstract. But it is not true in me; my hatred is
simply anger. That way also obscures my relationships with
others who make the work of the nature abusers possible.
These others are friends who will not discipline their lives to
do with less, who will not see that their comfort comes at
the expense of other humans, nature, and the future. In these
others I must include myself, for I profit daily. One friend
said it all when he stated, "Your electricity comes from a
nuclear plant."

Will Campbell's book helps me in this struggle. Challenged to give a ten-word definition of Christianity, Campbell answered in eight, "We're all bastards but God loves us
anyway." Later when a civil rights worker is murdered, the
definition comes back to haunt him. The same man who
goaded him into the definition applies it. "Which of these
two bastards does God love the most? Does he love the little
dead bastard, Jonathan [the murdered worker], the most? Or
does he love the living bastard, Thomas [the murderer] the
most?"

The whole point of redemption, the whole point of

God's love, is that the bastards will be/are reconciled. Justice is blown away by grace. Jonathan and Thomas eat the same supper, the same body of the Lord.

I don't find this easy. Grace offends me. I want to cry, "It isn't fair!" And I realize that my only hope is its unfairness. And I am not humbled, I am humiliated. My rage is shown for what it is, and I must repent.

What I don't understand is what, after I have repented, I must do, for I must act in this world for the preservation of both this world and the Gospel which must be spoken in it.

Campbell's reflections help. He wrote:

> I had become a doctrinaire social activist, without consciously choosing to be. And I would continue to be some kind of social activist. But there was a decided difference. Because from that point on I came to understand the nature of tragedy. And one who understands the nature of tragedy can never take sides. And I had taken sides . . . We did not understand that those we so vulgarly called "redneck" were part of the tragedy. They had been victimized. . . . They had their heads taken away by cunning, skillful, and well-educated gentlemen and ladies of the gentry.

He is talking about the way the economically vulnerable whites had been manipulated into hating the blacks to the advantage of a corrupt social system. Recognizing this, he ceased to take sides. He began going not only to the blacks with the gospel of reconciliation, but to the rednecks, to the Klan.

I can learn from his example: "We are all bastards but God loves us anyway." I own a house. It is heated half by wood I cut myself, half by natural gas. My electricity comes from nuclear energy. I have two credit cards, I own a car, and I put lots of miles on it. I am a white, middle-class consumer. A bastard. God loves me anyway. In response to that love, I must seek to love not only the creation which I have a natural inclination to love, but the bastards I live and work with. Love requires that I see their victimization by the system of economic and social oppression they seem to profit from. Love requires me to see that profit is an illusion, to see that we are all enslaved, that we are all in need of the liberating Gospel.

The siting commissioners are also victims. They are trapped by the very system they have created. Imagining themselves powerful men immune to the influence of the public, they must act like powerful men. They must act out their scenario of aggression. Claiming no alternatives can exist, they are slaves to their own imaginations, victims of the inevitable violence of their own willfulness. They are more to be pitied than hated.

MARCH 29

From the *World Book* my parents bought when I was in elementary school, I learned that our word *lent* comes from the old English word *lenten*, which means "spring," (the lengthening of days). It hardly seems up to bearing the burden of meaning it has come to have. It seems so pagan.

As I sit here this morning with nothing much on my mind, that seems OK. These woods are far from "church," far from the muttered words that contain the wildness of God. Here I sit on the edge between the domestic and the wild. Along the fence line I keep brush. Birds inhabit it and pass berry seeds. Brambles grow up. More birds come to them. Rabbits hide in them. In the summer deer bed down in their cover.

I walk near the brambles, choosing not to invade or destroy them for they are my access to lives not mine. And those lives are an access to the life of the Creator.

He is here revealing himself as surely as he reveals himself in words. But as I cannot seize the lives of the creatures, I cannot seize the life of the Creator. I must wait and let it occur about me. Wordlessly. Silently.

It is good.

MARCH 30

After two weeks of quiet, I am being turned back to activity. The commission has announced that it will try to gain access to the Caneadea site April 5—next Thursday. The expectation is that the confrontation will take place at my corner.

MARCH 31

Feelings have ceased. All internal mechanisms have shut down. I'm locked into the course of action that has been set, and all I can do is hope—I cannot even pray—that my heart was right, my motives as pure as possible, when I made my commitment.

One thought, however, does surface, a fear. Several Sundays ago, when I spoke to a gathering about nonviolence, I said the end of nonviolence was not victory. I said nonviolence was not opposition but a kind of wooing. When someone asked me if I really believed that our action could convert the siting commission, I was afraid to say yes. I was afraid that saying yes would be going too far, that if I said yes the questioner would laugh.

That moment keeps returning to me. I fear I do not believe what I affirm.

FIFTH SUNDAY IN LENT
APRIL FOOLS' DAY

A couple of weeks ago, when the siting commission sent its "information van" around the county, I struggled with how to respond. Some chose to demonstrate and pass out information. Some carried signs. Others blocked parking spaces so the van could not stop. On the last day of its visits, another group engaged it directly. They stuffed a dead skunk into its ventilation system. They poured buck scent on its carpet. They hung an effigy from its bumper, and they marched it out of town. Though their action actually hurt no one, it was violent. It had no redemptive qualities.

On the day the van came to Fillmore, I thought I would try something different. I determined to wear my arm band, buy coffee and donuts, and enter the van. I planned to say something like, "You come here intending to do violence to a land and people that I love. I intend to stand in your way, but I also intend you to know that I do not oppose you. I oppose only your action, and I invite you to see the violence of what you are engaged in and to join us in refusing to continue it." I didn't do it. I got to the scene and found nearly a hundred resisters had forced the van to park out of town. The long walk to it was too much for me. I rationalized, "There's no one in the van to influence. If I go, I'll be counted as a visit and be turned into a siting commission number to be used against me." Both rationalizations were true. But they shouldn't have mattered. I chickened out. I played Peter at the trial, and the cock has been crowing ever since.

These are hard thoughts for April Fools' Day. Another fool has crucified Christ.

APRIL 2

We met last night to go over the plans for Thursday. Before going to bed I read in Thomas Merton, "We are prisoners of a process, a dialectic of false promises and real deceptions leading to futility." It is that process we wish to break, that process of selling our *selves* for things.

Then the nightmares returned.

APRIL 4

From this morning's psalms:

The Lord will give strength unto his people;
the Lord will bless his people with peace. (29:11)

I will extol thee, O Lord, for thou hast lifted me up,
and hast not made my foes to rejoice over me.

O Lord, my God, I cried unto thee,
  and thou hast healed me. (30:1–2)

In thee, O Lord, do I put my trust;
  let me never be ashamed . . .
  deliver me speedily: be thou my strong rock, for an house
of defense to save me.
For thou art my rock and my fortress;
  therefore for thy name's sake lead me and guide me.
Pull me out of the net that they have laid privily for me:
  for thou art my strength.
Into thine hand I commit my spirit:
  thou hast redeemed me, O Lord God of truth. (31:1–5)

I recognize that these verses are not promises. Reading them this morning does not mean that tomorrow I will not be arrested, that tomorrow the people of Allegany County will prevail. I know that the Lord's ways are mysterious, and that his will is not my will. At best I sometimes will his will. That is what I'm trying to do now. The thing I take from these is the assurance that he is my strength and that all I must offer is my faithfulness, my willing myself into his hands. I do that. And so, while I may fear for the moment, I do not fear for his purposes or my part in them.

As I look at the planned action and my part in it, I wonder at how it has come to be. Quiet, nonconfrontational me, the fool on the hill, the poet in the woods, lining up to face down the state police, the whole marshalled forces of the State of New York. Just saying no. I think I have come to this by obedience, and I think this obedience will change my life. Having come to this point of commitment, how can I retreat without giving up the truths I have embraced? I cannot. The earth is the Lord's. Standing for it, I stand for its Creator and proclaim Christ has come to redeem his own. All shall be well.

APRIL 5

I woke at 3:00 A.M. from a nightmare. In it the police had somehow circled around our barrier and were behind us. Aggressively, without making distinctions or reading the injunction, they began to arrest spectators. I had to get up, make toast, and drink a glass of orange juice to shake the oppressiveness of the dream, to compose myself so I could sleep again.

APRIL 6

The morning began as we planned. I went to the bridge at 7:30, met the other monitors and the six grandparents who were to form the first line of resistance. Cars streamed past us, heading for the gathering spot at the German Settlement Church near the site. The numbers encouraged us. At 9 o'clock, two resisters locked a chain to one side of the bridge and placed plywood on the open deck so chairs could be set up. Another climbed into the steelwork and tied a large flag directly overhead, others moved farm equipment to the end of the bridge: a disk, a large tractor, and a wood wagon.

When word reached us by radio that the siting team was about five miles away, the chain was pulled across the bridge and locked. The grandparents moved forward, took their chairs, and handcuffed themselves to the chain. Behind them, resisters unfurled a large banner, GRANDPARENTS FOR THE FU-TURE. The bridge was closed with the farm equipment, and one hundred demonstrators moved into place. When Sheriff Scholes arrived with the "walk-over" team and state troop-ers, he greeted the grandparents and treated them with the respect he has treated everyone with so far. After a few mo-ments of conversation, he retreated to discuss the situation with the troopers. He returned, had the injunction read, and when the grandparents refused to move, called the troopers. When they arrived, Alexandra Landis, an eighty-seven-year-old Harvard Ph.D., presented the sheriff with the flag that had covered the coffin of her son, a World War II flyer.

Then the arrests began. As they proceeded, the resisters staged a slow march up the hill toward the next road block, a five-bottom plow dragged across the road. There I met Melissa, my daughter. She had been serving food three miles away, but curiosity had overcome her. We stood and talked, waiting for what would come. An hour later the sheriff, the "walk-over" team and the troopers again approached the resisters. Once more a deputy read the injunction. Then ev-erything changed. The troopers formed a phalanx (there were about forty of them), moved around the barrier, and marched into the crowd, scattering it as it tried to move backward in an orderly fashion. In this confusion Melissa and I were separated.

The troopers moved aggressively forward. Since I was on the radio and could not afford to risk arrest so early in the action, I hiked through six-inch snow in the fields along the road. I could not keep up with the front of the line, so I deliberately dropped back to keep track of the arrests and relayed what I witnessed to the base radio.

The troopers arrested at random. They took retreating

protestors from behind, and they took spectators from the side of the road. They made no distinctions between people blocking the road and people watching. It was my nightmare in the waking world.

As the phalanx moved ahead, the distance the troopers had to walk arrestees increased. They made fewer arrests. Their intent seemed to be to disrupt the organization of the protest and to create as much uncertainty as they could. Nothing in their actions seemed to be directed toward calming anxiety or stabilizing the situation. With my radio I stood off to the side, observing like a dispassionate writer, narrating what I saw for those ahead of me. Only today in my exhaustion do I realize how passionately I was involved.

As I approached a crest I could not see over, another observer, Minnow, came on the radio, "A group on horseback is coming," he said. "They're approaching the troopers. They've stopped. The troopers have stopped. The troopers are trying to push them back. The horses are backing. Now they're turning around. The troopers are among them. A trooper is trying to grab a horse.

"The troopers have drawn nightsticks."

A wave of sickness hit me. Oh God! I thought, not this. Where's Melissa! Please don't let her be there. I began to run forward.

Minnow continued, his voice sharpening, "They're hitting a horse. They're hitting a rider."

"They're dragging him from the horse. They've pulled him off. They're beating him. They have him on the ground."

About that time I came over the crest and could see the action ahead of me. Most of the troopers were still in a rough block. Ahead of them, the horses were still or circling slowly.

Then two troopers led a prisoner past me. He seemed to be holding his hand, and one of the troopers was asking him about it. A horse and rider approached them and sidestepped a few paces away. The troopers threatened the rider, who hassled them verbally and then retreated.

As I scanned the group of demonstrators, which was fragmented, stunned, and largely silent, I saw Melissa off to one side, standing in the woods. She was not alone. I went up to her and touched her gently on the shoulder. She turned, and I held her. "I can't believe what I just saw," she said. The person with her greeted me and raised her mask. A friend. Her husband was missing, and she wanted to know if he'd been arrested. He had.

We stood together watching the dwindling group of protestors mill about the troopers. Then the troopers gathered, turned, and began a slow march back down the road. The confrontation was over.

PALM SUNDAY

I object to the nuclear industry on two grounds. First, it abuses the earth; it destroys. And second, it concentrates power in the hands of a few technocrats who then determine the fate of both the earth and the creatures of the earth. This concentration is evident in the attitude the siting commission has taken toward the people of Allegany County. From the beginning they have assured us that we are incompetent to make our own decisions, that we haven't the information necessary. Every time someone disagrees, no matter what his qualifications, the siting commission simply says, "Trust us, we know the truth." Disagreement is defined as ignorance.

A particular example of this is Orazzio's inflammatory rhetoric. He speaks the world as he wishes it to be, without considering the truth. Without seeking to learn anything about the senior citizens who handcuffed themselves to the bridge, he called them dupes and victims of cynical leaders. Three of the six are Ph.D.'s, one in chemistry.

I write this on a day given to remembering the triumphant entry of Christ into Jerusalem. This year the day seems empty and abstract. The events of the week are too overpowering. The knowledge that Christ's entry led directly to his Crucifixion looms too dark ahead. This seems the strangest holiday of the year, a celebration of a misunderstanding. In this world the Kingdom has not yet come, though our hearts long for it and our lives incline toward it.

APRIL 9

Holy Week begins, and I near the end of this journal. I am glad for both. For forty-one days now I've been beating out words, thinking, thinking, thinking about my every action, and I am tired. I wonder what good all these words have done. I know nothing now that I did not know at the beginning—except the deviousness of my own mind and heart. I set out to explore the meaning of the redemption of creation. I've failed. I've explored only my wandering thoughts, my errant emotions: anger, sorrow, occasional joy. I've come to think that the meaning of the redemption of creation cannot be explored; it must rather be worked out in living relationships. In tending to stewardship responsibilities, in living in

Christ, we live in the process of redemption. Living within it, we cannot comment objectively, for the redemption of creation is an idea larger even than personal salvation.

The earth is the Lord's. He has chosen to risk it by giving it over to human stewardship. No matter how I try, I shall never be more than a bumbling gardener. The events of last Thursday, and my inability to put them behind me, have sobered me.

Had I the day to do over, given the same knowledge I had, I would do it again. Going forward with the knowledge I now have, both about the institutions of power and their willingness to use force, and my own responses, I can only pray that at the next moment of decision, I will have grace and wisdom, for at that moment my present knowledge will be as insufficient as my past knowledge was.

APRIL 11

As I ponder these last few days, I think that perhaps this struggle is more appropriate to Holy Week than I first thought.

What was the crowd that cheered Christ's triumphant ride into Jerusalem thinking? They expected a king who would free them from Roman oppression. I cannot dismiss their expectations and criticize their lack of spiritual discernment. Christ fooled everyone. And I wonder what that crowd thought when he reached Jerusalem and began to go about his business. In that week he cast out the money changers and silenced the priests and scribes with conundrums. His followers must have believed something great was about to happen. After all, the Jewish story is the story of the exodus, the story of political liberation. It is only Christians, looking backward, who focus on the creation/fall story, who see redemption and restoration—forgiveness of sins—as the central story of God's dealing with humans.

What do I make of the conflicting implications of these stories? What do I say, after a month of praying the Psalms with their talk, their unending talk, of enemies and victories over enemies? Why should I not be thinking of victory over oppressors? Why should I be thinking of giving myself up to be crucified?

I simply do not know.

I return always to obedience. I must be obedient to my call to be a steward. I find where that takes me as I go forward, carried both by intention and circumstance. My hope remains in Christ, in grace. It is lost in mystery.

MAUNDY THURSDAY

I sit listening to the wind, adjusting my mind to the quiet of this place. But I am not alone.

I bring with me to this place the presences of others. Today I bring with me those I sat with at the noon communion service, those friends I have worshipped with so many years, those friends from whom I take the comfort of the presence of Christ, those friends in whose presence I feel I am home.

With those and others I went forward. I broke from the loaf, held out for me, a crust and dipped it in the wine. I ate the body and blood of Christ. And I returned to my seat, my eyes filled with tears, my spirit filled with joy, with a sense of Christ present in the room, with the sense of belonging, with the knowledge of my membership in his body burning in my throat.

And then I came here. To be alone. But not alone. Never alone, for the union transcends the short distances I have placed between myself and others.

This morning I read Katherine Paterson's essay, "Heart in Hiding." In it she writes:

> I don't think morality is the basic theme of the Bible. I think its theme is closer to what physicists would call beauty. By itself, morality is not beautiful enough. Listen to Genesis: "And God said, Let there be light: and there was light. And God saw the light, that it was good: . . . And God saw everything that he had made, and behold, it was very good." The word "good" is not a moral judgment, but an aesthetic one. God saw that what he had made was very beautiful.
>
> . . . But the Bible says something more: that the posture of the eternal Creator toward the finite creation is that of good will. Listen . . . to Gerard Manley Hopkins:

> *The world is charged with the grandeur of God.*
> *It will flame out, like shining from shook foil;*
> *It gathers to a greatness, like the ooze of oil*
> *Crushed . . .*

As I sit here the world *is charged* with the grandeur of God. It is by that grandeur that he woos me. It is by that grandeur that I know my unworthiness. And it is by that grandeur that I come to grace for that grandeur is grace. It is the presence of

Christ in this world, moving to restore the wholeness of that morning when God said that it was good.

It is this vision that enlivens hope in me. It is this vision that makes me a servant of all that is.

What will come of our efforts to halt the siting of a dump in this valley, I do not know. I do not need to know. But this I do know: Christ is in the world, redeeming the world, and I will name myself Christ's man as long as I have breath to breathe his name.

GOOD FRIDAY

I ended yesterday's journal entry so positively. Then for no reason, as I drove down the hill into the valley, the memory of an unspeakable crime I'd heard narrated on a television talk show woke in me, and my imagination went wild.

Is crucifixion required? I don't know, but it is a fact. What kind of God do I affirm?

APRIL 14

I think this will be the last entry in this journal. How can I end a journey through Lent on Saturday? How can I stop when Christ lies in the tomb? All that is literary in me, all that believes and wants to testify to the Resurrection wants to go on. Yet the action of this journal, the movement in time toward a resolution of the one issue dominating the thought of this county is in suspension. The siting commission has not withdrawn. Their spokeswoman made very clear yesterday that they do not intend to withdraw.

Yesterday in my reading I came across a story about Archbishop Desmond Tutu. He reportedly said something about God being present in events, but not nearly obviously enough to satisfy Archbishop Tutu's need to see him clearly. I read the passage to my wife, Linda, and said, "That's the way I feel."

She answered, "You aren't paying attention."

Perhaps I'm not. Perhaps I haven't eyes to see. I once received a letter from one of my readers who told me she was praying for me to meet the Lord because I sounded as if I really wanted to know him. What can I say? Where does all this leave me?

After the Good Friday service yesterday, I met Jim Wolfe, a biologist friend. We drove up to Pike to a Free Methodist camp where he is studying a small lake fed by water diverted from Wiscoy Creek.

We took a canoe and paddled to the inlet where Jim took a water sample. Temperature: 46 degrees. PH: 5.0. I was cold. The wind blew harshly over the open water, and I wished for my gloves, but as I held the canoe steady against the wind and Jim marked his sample, I thought on the contrast of my unsettledness in the past few days and my calm on the water.

We crossed the lake to the outlet where a Canada goose swam about, ignoring us, sampled the water there, and then returned to the dock. The camp director met us and we talked. The study Jim is doing is a result of an increased algae growth in the lake. Campers no longer want to swim in it. To combat the algae the camp owners plan to release sterile carp in the lake to eat it. The study is necessary to complete the permit process.

The plans sounded fine, but just before we left, the director asked about using copper sulfate to kill the algae. It seems the local Agway recommended that to keep the lake clean for swimming before the carp are established. Jim was very quiet, and I sensed what was troubling him. The copper sulfate would work. It would kill the algae, but the algae would then settle to the bottom, decompose, and use up the oxygen in the water. That in turn might cause a fishkill. He said so.

Unspoken in this conversation was the hard question, the question that lies behind all stewardship issues: What's more important, the fish population or an algae-free lake for swimmers? What's more important, a harmonious living within the bounds of nature or a technological fix allowing us to do what we want now?

I tell this story because it is our story at this point in time. We face it with nuclear energy. We face it with coal-fired plants. We face it with plastics, toxins, and automobiles. "Forward to the Pleistocene," say the Earth Firsters. While I can't quite say that, part of me would like to. What I must say is forward to a new sense of stewardship, to a greater inclusiveness in our caring.

I know where I am. I am here at Remnant Acres, trying my best to live responsibly, to care for the small portion of earth God has given directly to my care. It gives me great joy to be here, to do his will. If it takes me beyond this place to the other side of the valley to stand between the siting commission and the land, I will go. If it takes me to jail, I will go.

But I hope it takes me to neither of those places. I hope it takes me right here to the faith that keeps the mountains in place. And I hope it takes me deeper and deeper into the community that dwells here.

As I came up Tucker Hill, about a quarter-mile before my turnoff on School Farm Road, I spotted a deer, a doe feeding in the field. I stopped the car, reached into the backseat for my binoculars, and settled down to watch her. She was turned away from me, her tail a dark black stripe lined with a fringe of white, flattened against her rump. I could see her head through her legs as she grazed. The legs seemed too thin to hold her weight, and they splayed out a bit as she bent to reach the grass.

At one point she suddenly straightened. Her head came up, and then her ears, edged with black, stood tense. She glanced about, then returned to feeding. I watched her five minutes before she straightened again, looked across the field and then bounded slowly over a rise. I waited for her to appear going up the other side, but she did not. I figured she was following the cover of the little hollow to the trees, so I put the car in gear and pulled forward to look down it. Two other deer grazed with her.

Not wanting to scare them, I kept moving up the hill. I turned in on School Farm Road and stopped the car. I took my glasses and got out. In the biting wind I stood watching them graze.

Perhaps it is because of them I can end this journal here. "One world at a time," Thoreau said as he neared death. Thoreau was wrong. Hopkins was right. We have both worlds at once. This world is "charged with the grandeur of God."

PASSION SUNDAY

Virginia Stem Owens

At church this morning, the
Fifth Sunday of Lent and the last before Palm Sunday, the
bishop confirmed nineteen young people, mostly junior high
school students. The girls, in their new spring dresses, were
taller than most of the boys, who haven't gotten their adoles-
cent growth spurt yet. Their adult sponsors stood to one side
while the bishop, round and red in his chimere, laid his hands
on the heads of the young confirmands, one by one, and
asked the Lord to strengthen, empower, and sustain them for
all the days of their lives. Family members beamed from the
pews. A kind of nimbus, the lingering shreds from the clouds

of glory that still trail young adolescents, colored their cheeks and glinted off their downcast lashes.

Merciful heavens, I thought, remembering my own very impressionable self at that age, how fine they must think life is at this moment. These young people still actually believe in the possibility of living up to the promise of their new clothes. They were so fetching, even their glowing relatives might be forgiven for their own high hopes for these youngsters today.

But the rest of us, I noticed, not so personally caught up in the emotion of the moment, smiled somewhat knowingly at one another, as though to say, *well, of course, everyone feels proud and happy today, but . . . give them time. Wait till the bloom rubs off. They'll find that we all, unfortunately, are made of the same clay.*

Not that we articulated those words precisely. It was just the way we smiled. Knowingly. With the knowledge of good and evil.

This afternoon, having changed my own Sunday clothes for jeans, I went hiking in the state park. The "interpretive" part of the trail had recently been renovated after long neglect. The numbered posts that had long ago lost their identification markers now had new little essays, encased in Lucite, attached to them, informing hikers about the more common species of trees, vines, and bushes. I read them all as I went along, noting particularly the errors in spelling and punctuation. These were the work, the message on the last post declared, of Barry Nelson, an Eagle Scout. "I would like to thank the Texas Parks and Wildlife Department Rangers," he wrote, "for their time and expertice in helping me with my Project."

One of the plants identified was the palmetto, a plant that, as the diminutive form indicates, is low to the ground, having no trunk. The stem and leaves grow directly out of the marshy soil. It's the kind of palm we used to wave on Palm Sunday mornings in the country Baptist churches I knew as a child. Today, however, any church that can possibly afford them uses store-bought or mail-order palm fronds that come from actual trees, not the lowly palmetto. After you've used it on Palm Sunday morning, you're supposed to fold it into a cross for Good Friday. All you get, though, is one puny sliver, more like a giant grass blade than a branch, one to a customer.

Often we have a procession too. A few years ago at my church we were herded into the parking lot and then marched around the building in single file, singing the processional hymn and clutching our scrap of palm. Our voices sounded thin, the way singing usually does outdoors. I have to say, it was a pretty poor imitation of what we later read about in the Gospel lesson. About on the same ratio as a spindly palm frond to a full palmetto branch.

But then, I have to admit that I've always felt pretty ambivalent about Palm Sunday. And I suspect this is probably true of most steady churchgoers, the ones familiar enough with Passion Week to know what comes next. In fact, the Gospel reading for Palm Sunday itself covers not just the parade into Jerusalem, but everything clear through the Crucifixion. The regulars know this and consequently are careful not to get too giddy out in the parking lot because what comes next isn't a pretty story. We never really feel like we can cut loose, as those first Palm Sunday paraders did. Because we already know, as Paul Harvey says, *the rest of the story.* It's hard to put your whole heart into the triumphal entry of Jesus into Jerusalem when you're dreading the ignominious part you're to play next.

105

So all the adults hold back, waving our thin green feather weakly and singing "Hosanna" thinly into the open and accusing air. We push the small children out in front and cravenly encourage them to act out the jubilation we know will shortly be overshadowed by our shame. Trapped again within our knowledge of good and evil.

For what we know is that on Good Friday somebody's going to be sticking a nail instead of a palm frond in our hand and telling us to march up the aisle to the front and, with a hammer lying there, pound the nail into a rickety wooden facsimile of a cross. And somehow we think if we don't get too exuberant with the palm frond on Sunday, maybe we can escape the nail on Friday. Our complicity in the Crucifixion won't count as much, won't actually do any damage, if we refuse to shout and sing in the parade. If our part in the joy is smaller, it only seems reasonable we'll get a correspondingly smaller portion of the scalding humiliation reserved for the fickle crowd. That's one of the problems of being grown up, with reading ahead and knowing the rest of the story. It gets harder to throw yourself into the moment. The knowledge of the looming evil cancels the present joy.

Actually, only one of the Gospels, John's, identifies as palms the trees the people stripped on the road into Jerusalem. The other writers just say the people lopped branches off the trees and strewed them in the way. Along with their clothes. (I am living for the day they make us disrobe in the parking lot. I have been at public gatherings where people got so excited they stripped off their clothes, but that was twenty or more years ago, and the excitement wasn't about Jesus.)

Still, that's the point of Palm Sunday, isn't it—or wasn't it, before we got so knowledgeable? To get excited about Jesus? Leaping and dancing and shouting and raising Cain because your dearest dreams are going to come true, your fondest hopes about to be realized? What if those original enthusiasts were a little off the mark? What if they did think Jesus was going to overthrow the government or make them all rich and healthy or throw the rascals out of the Temple? At least their hopes and dreams were the sort they could get excited about, that could make them shout and sing. If you want a contemporary parallel to their excitement, think of the way people who win the sweepstakes today act, shrieking and jumping up and down. I know; winning the sweepstakes doesn't sound particularly high minded. But what *would* it take to make you jump up and down in glee?

Or even beam broadly? Those proud relatives sitting in the pews this morning, for instance, about to bust their buttons, certainly had hope shining in their eyes. And the young girls and boys were conscious of all the eyes on them, of something important happening to them at that moment, rushing by them so quickly they could scarcely comprehend the light glancing off the surface of it. For that matter, I could even imagine a flourish of exuberance in the Eagle Scout as he attached that last Lucite tablet to the post there in the woods—blissfully unaware that some curmudgeon would one day be criticizing his spelling and punctuation.

So what if we know that, by the time they're in college, the nineteen new confirmands may not be coming to church anymore. So what if we can predict that, for a certain percentage of them, whoever makes their funeral arrangements one day will be surprised to discover they were once members of St. James Church. "Maybe we ought to have an Episcopal priest do the service," they'll say with a shrug. So what?

But then what bridal pair, saying their vows in a trembling haze of intensity, foresees the pain they will one day cause one another? What mother, having her new child delivered into her arms for the first time, dwells on the grief and anguish that little lump will cause her? What believer on his confirmation day realizes how many times he will embrace—rather than renounce—Satan and all the spiritual forces of wickedness that rebel against God, even though today he swears he will not? And what citizen of Jerusalem, waving his palm branch, throwing down his clothes for the donkey to step on, knew he would be shouting "Crucify!" in a few more days?

None. Yet each of us knows on Palm Sunday, as we accept the frond thrust into our hands, that before the world has turned around one more time, we will have betrayed, denied, witnessed either falsely or not at all. And so we are ashamed.

So what? The parade is not to honor us anyway.

At its best, the rest of our earthly life is going to be one long Palm Sunday, a procession of praise and great expectations in the face of certain failure—or it's going to be nothing. A resignation to futility. Our excitement is always going to be slightly out of focus, through a glass darkly. What we bless today, we betray tomorrow. Such is the cycle of human life.

Nevertheless, despite this, maybe even *because* of this, we must take our place in the parade. Must constantly relive our baptisms, renew our vows, no matter how often broken. The knowledge of his goodness must sweep away the knowledge of our own evil, as rushing water sweeps away debris. Aware of our own wavering natures, we must declare *this is it! Heaven is passing by at this moment!*

We will never be worthy of our new confirmation clothes, but he is. That's why we strip them off and lay them before him. Even his donkey's hoofprint glorifies them. If it's ever going to be—that glory and hallelujah in our hearts—it must be now! We can't wait to be worthy or the stones would have to do our work for us. Our hearts, however scarred and wary, must give way once more to sweet anticipation. Rush out. Grab whatever lies to hand. Wave it. Shout. Proclaim blessed the one who comes in the name of the Lord!

PALM SUNDAY

Robert Siegel

A Colt, the Foal of an Ass

*Creation itself will be set free . . . and obtain the glorious
liberty of the children of God.*

Contemplating the dust he stands
in the direct unbearable noon, tethered
to the dead thorn. His long ears hang
down, twitch and revolve as the gang of flies
brassily land, bite, and ascend
in a constant small black cloud. His hide

at each bite quivers and smooths out
like this earthquake-tormented land
while his tail, with its bathrobe tassel, larrups
and swats too late.
                    His eyes, half-lidded
in the bleaching light, are fixed and still,
his plain dull face perpendicular as a post,
his forelock hanging over it.
                              He does not
turn toward the stranger who stands talking
with the two at the door. Only his muzzle,
soft as silk and still faintly pink,
twitches as his nostrils catch the foreign scent,
widen and lift his lip for half a second.
                                          Then
lazily he turns to look, eyes glazed, indifferent,
tugs at the harsh rope once, desists,
patient with donkey patience, already learning
the rough discipline that pulled him from the grass
and his mother's side.
                       Now, without warning,
as if he feels a tremor underfoot
some inaudible alarm from the world's core,
he bares his teeth and breaks the air with a sound
like a stone wrenched and crying from its center,
harsh and grating as a rusty hinge
on which the whole earth hangs.
                                Later
there is a moment with a crowd roaring
in surges long and hoarse as breakers crashing,
cool green plants to tread over the hot stones
and flowers which offer a brief fragrance underhoof—

111

one moment of all those in the years that are to come
of fetching and hauling for masters bad and good,
when he does not mind what he is carrying,
when a sense of joy returns, the early smell
of grass while he first stood, unsteady in the field
with a beast's dim sense of liberty.

Still, he cannot guess what he is carrying,
and will not remember this moment in all the years
until he is worn out, lame,
until the hammer is brought down on his
   unsuspecting head,
his hooves melted to glue, his hide thrown to the
   crows,
when he shall return to this now, this always
he continues to live in,
this moment of bearing the man,
a weight that is light and easy,
celebrated in a rough, ecstatic chorus,
toward his own fatal burden heavier than the world.

MAUNDY THURSDAY

~

Walter Wangerin, Jr.

How young I was at the period of my crisis, I do not remember. Young enough to crawl beneath the pews. Short enough to stand up on the seats of pews, when the congregation arose to sing hymns, and still be hidden. Old enough to hold womanhood in awe, but much too young to tease women. Old enough to want to see Jesus. Young enough to believe that the mortal eye *could* see Jesus.

I wanted to see Jesus. There was the core of my crisis. I mean, see him as eyewitnesses are able to see: his robe and the rope at his waist, his square, strong hands, the sandals on his feet, his tumble of wonderful hair, and the love in his eyes, deep love in his eyes—for me!

For it seemed to me in those days that everyone else in my church must be seeing him on a regular basis and that I alone was denied the sight of my Lord. They were a contented people, confident and unconcerned. I, on the other hand, I felt like a little Cain among the Christians, from whom the dear Lord Jesus chose to hide particularly. No one seemed to tremble in the Holy House of the Lord. But I . . .

Well, the knowledge of my peculiar exile came all in a rush one Sunday, when the preacher was preaching a mumblin' monotone of a sermon. One sentence leaped from his mouth and seized me: "We were eyewitnesses," he said. Eyewitnesses. We! I sat straight up and tuned my ear. This seemed, suddenly, the special ability of a special people to which the preacher belonged: to be eyewitnesses. Who's this *we*? What did they see? I glanced at my mother beside me, whose expression was not one of astonishment. Evidently, eyewitnessing was familiar stuff to her. She was one of the *we*. I took a fast survey of the faces behind me. Sleepy-eyed, dull-eyed, thoughtful-eyed; but no one's eyes were dazzled. None widened in wonder at what the preacher said. So then, they all belonged to the *we*: eyewitnesses, every one of them! "We," the preacher was saying, "have seen the majesty of Jesus . . ."

No!

I didn't say that out loud. But I thought it very loud.

No, but I haven't! This was a stinging realization. *I haven't seen Jesus! My eyes were never witnesses!*

All at once the stained-glass picture of a praying Jesus wasn't enough for me. The Jesuses in my Sunday-school

114

books were merely pictures and a kind of mockery. I did not doubt that the Lord Jesus was actually there in his house somewhere—but where?

Even before the preacher was finished preaching, I dropped to the floor and peered through a forest of ankles, front and back and side to side—seeking Jesus perhaps on his hands and knees, a Jesus crawling away from me in a robe and a rope. But I saw nothing unusual and earned nothing for my effort except the disapproval of my mother, who hauled me up by my shoulder, but who probably wouldn't understand my panic since she was one of the *we*.

For the rest of that service I sought in the faces around me some anxiety to match my anxious heart. But everyone sang the hymns with a mindless ease. I searched my memory for some dim moment when I might have caught a glimpse of Jesus. There was none. No, he'd never appeared to me. But he must be here, for hadn't he appeared to these others? Then why would he hide from me? Did he hate me? And where, in this temple of the Lord, would he be hiding?

Thus, my crisis.

Sunday after Sunday I looked for Jesus. I ransacked the rooms of a very large church. I acquainted myself with kitchens and closets and boiler rooms—checking for half-eaten sandwiches, a vagrant sandal, signs of the skulking Lord.

One Sunday, exactly when the preacher stood chanting the liturgy at the altar, I experienced a minor revelation. It seemed to me that the bold bass voice of the chant was not the preacher's at all, whose speaking voice was rather nasal and whining. It seemed that someone else was singing instead. For the preacher faced away from us, and the altar was as long as a man is tall, and the wooden altar (ah-ha!) was built in the shape of a monstrous coffin. Therefore, the real singer was lying inside the altar. And who else would that secret singer be—but Jesus?

I kept a shrewd eye on the altar for the rest of the service, to be sure that he didn't escape. And after the service I took my heart in my hands and crept into the chancel, crept right up to the altar, certain that the Christ was still reclining therein, waiting in his tomb, as it were, till all the people departed.

Suddenly—*Ah-ha!*—I popped round to the back of the altar and peered inside its hollow cavity and saw . . . not Jesus. I saw a broken chair, a very old hymnal, and dust, dust, dust as thick as the centuries of human toil and misery.

For my restless soul there was no peace. I was not suffering a crisis of faith; never once did I doubt the truth or the presence of Jesus. Mine was a crisis of love—or perhaps of knowledge. Either the Lord had decided to avoid me particularly, or else I was stupid, the only one who did not know in which room the dear Lord Jesus abided. There must be one holier than all other rooms, one room so sacred and terrible that no one mentioned it, except in whispers and elders' meetings. Not the preacher's office. Dreadful as that room was, I'd already scouted it. Not the sacristy, nor the loft for the organ pipes, nor the choir room (which smelled of human sweat). A holiest of holies, a . . .

All at once I knew which room! My heart leaped into my throat with joy and fear at once. It was a room whose door I passed ever with a tingling hush, whose mysterious interior I had never seen. Horrified by my own bravery, but desperate to see my Jesus, I determined to venture the door of that room, and to enter.

And so it came to pass that, during a particular worship

service, during a very long sermon, I claimed the privilege of children and left my mother in the pew and crept downstairs all by myself to The Forbidden Room, the only room left where Jesus could be hiding: The Women's Rest Room.

Oh, how hot my poor face burned at my own audacity, at the danger I was daring. If the holiest place of the temple in old Jerusalem might kill an unworthy priest, how would this room of taboos receive a little boy? I swallowed and panted and sweat. But I wanted to see Jesus. I lifted my hand and I knocked.

"Jesus? Are you in there?"

No answer. None.

So I screwed my little courage together, and I sucked a breath, and I pushed on the door, and it actually opened.

"Hello? Hello? Jesus—?"

I do not remember whether that was on a Maundy Thursday. It might well have been. It should have been.

With a deep, funereal gloom I returned to my mother. With a deathly sense of finalities I took the pew beside her. I was as woeful as any disciple who heard the Lord say, "I am leaving you, and where I go you cannot come." Abandoned!

Jesus does not abide in women's rest rooms. Mirrors are there, surrounded by lights and suffused by incense. But not Jesus.

Jesus was nowhere in this church for me.

I was a most sorrowful disciple. *Lord? Is it I? Did I somehow betray you that you would leave me alone in the night?*

With grim, remorseful eyes I watched the service proceed. Perhaps my senses were intensified by sorrow, for I saw things as I had not seen them before. Things moved

117

slowly, burdened by unusual weight and meaning. The preacher—far, far in the front of the church, robed in black and white—was lifting bread and mumbling. Then he was lifting an enormous cup and mumbling some more, mysterious words I was likely never to understand: ". . . this cup is the New Testament in my blood . . ."

Blood. That seemed a grave word altogether.

"Do this," he was murmuring, "in remembrance of me."

Then people began to arise and to file forward. There was the deep timbre of song all around me. People were devout. Incomprehensible things were happening.

Then my mother got up. In marvelous docility, she walked forward down the aisle, away from me. My mother is a strong woman. She could haul me from the ground in one hand. This humility, then, was strange, and I stood up on the pew to watch her.

Far in the front of the church my mother diminished, almost to the size of a child. And then, to my astonishment, she did childish things: She kneeled down. She bowed her head. She let the preacher feed her! This was my mother, who knew how to make *me* eat! Like a little baby, she let the preacher lower the cup to her lips and give her a drink. And then she stood, and they bowed to each other; and almost, as it were, upon a cushion of air my mother floated back to me.

Oh, this was a different woman. My mighty mother seemed infinitely soft.

And when she sat beside me and lowered her head to pray, I actually *smelled* the difference too. She had returned in a cloud of sweetness. I tasted this exquisite scent deep in my throat, and like a puppy found myself sniffing closer and closer to my mother's face—for the odor was arising from her nostrils, from her breathing, from within her.

Suddenly she looked up to see my face just inches from hers.

"What's the matter?" she whispered, and a whole bouquet of the odor overwhelmed me.

"Mama!" I breathed in wonder. "What's that?"

She wrinkled her forehead. "What's what?" she said with frankincense.

"That," I said. I wanted to tug at her mouth. "That smell. What do I smell?"

"What I drank."

"But what is it? What's inside you?"

She began to flip for a hymn in the hymnal. "Oh, Wally," she said casually, "that's Jesus. It's Jesus inside of me."

Jesus!

My mother then joined the congregation in singing a hymn with a hundred verses. But I kept standing on the pew beside her and grinning and grinning at her profile. *Jesus!* I put out my hand and rested it on my mother's shoulder. She glanced up, saw that my face was exploding with grins, gave me a pat and a smile, then went back to singing.

But *Jesus!* She told me where Jesus was at! Not far away from me at all. Closer to me than I ever thought possible. In my mama! He never had been hiding. I'd been looking wrong. My mighty mother was his holy temple all along.

So I shocked her by throwing my arms around her neck and hugging her with the gladness of any disciple who has seen the Lord alive again.

So she hauled my little self down to the pew beside her and commanded silliness to cease, but I didn't mind. A boy can grin as silently as the sky.

And so it was that two commands of our Lord, delivered on Maundy Thursday, the night before he died, were twined into one for me. "Do this," he said of his Holy Supper, "in remembrance of me"—and in so doing his death and his presence would be proclaimed to all the world. My mother did it; she ate and drank; and as her faith received her Savior truly, she bore the Lord in my direction, and I met him in her.

And the second command was this: "Love one another." My mama did that too. And so there were two disciples side by side on the same pew. And one of them was grinning.

GOOD FRIDAY

~

Virginia Stem Owens

Although it has not happened since 1913 and won't happen again till 2008, Easter can come as early as March 23, just barely inside the official limits of spring. But whether Holy Week falls in March or April makes little difference in Texas. It's always springtime here by then.

People like the dogwood to be in full bloom for Good Friday. They like to point out to one another how the dogwood's white blossom, shaped like an ivory Maltese cross, each point dented and tinged with red, is an emblem of Christ's crucifixion wounds. They even send one another greeting cards bearing the so-called Legend of the Dogwood, which links the tree with the wood used for the cross.

The dogwood trees are usually blooming at about the same time I teach college sophomores the Housman poem that begins,

Loveliest of trees, the cherry now
Is hung with bloom along the bough,
And stands about the woodland ride
Wearing white for Eastertide.

Most of my students have never seen cherry trees in bloom. The Texas weather is too mild and genial for the cherry's hearty nature, so I rely on the dogwood tree to furnish them with a reasonable facsimile of Housman's vision. The decorative dogwood chooses to display its white blossoms along the highways precisely when they will be the most conspicuous—before their own leaves unfurl and before the other, taller trees have put on their new leaves. Thus, the shadowy recesses of the winter-bare forests provide the perfect background for the white blossoms.

The only rival to the dogwood's ostentation during Holy Week is the redbud, also known as "the Judas tree." Most flowering trees bloom only from the tips of their twigs, but the redbud's small, purplish pink blossoms pop out all over its smooth, silvery skin, even directly from the branches and the trunk. A popular horticulturist calls the redbud "the colorful doll of our hardwood forests" and compares its flowers to "little dancing shoes."

People in this part of Texas consider a perfect Holy Week one in which the dogwood's dramatic appearance exactly overlaps the redbud's rouging of the Texas roadsides with its smudges of pink. And as if the native flowering trees weren't enough, bluebonnets smear across acres of pastureland like mosaics of lapis lazuli, punctuated by saffron Indian paintbrush.

They are very beautiful, these blossom-laden trees and fields of blowing flowers, heartbreakingly beautiful. And I have plenty of opportunity to have my heart broken as I drive twice a week to the university, 60 miles away. The little two-lane highway dips and twists over creeks and around farms that used to grow cotton but now are grazed by crossbred cattle.

Some of the descendants of the people who used to pick the cotton still live along this road or in the tiny towns of Shiro and Roan's Prairie. Their decrepit houses lean and gape at the surrounding woods and fields. They stay, the people who live in these hungry houses, because they are tied to the dogwood and redbud, just as surely as they were once tied to the cotton. Every spring they wait for the dogwood's appearing, and its glory, sudden and stunning, gets them through another year. So they stay on in their obliquely slanting houses, sustained by social security or ADC checks, rather than move to the city.

I suppose I'm one of the few people who actually *like* Lent. I like it in the same way I like throwing away last year's student essays and clearing out my file cabinets. During Lent some deep crack opens in my soul, down which I like to shovel the dirt and debris that has accumulated over the year. The sly self-deceptions, the dogged willfulness, the witless pain I've left in my wake that I've been too busy to notice or repair. From back in February, before the blooming starts, forty days always looks like little enough time for this task. The penitential season is for clearing away accumulated garbage, and I usually set to work with a will.

But three years ago, late in March, I was driving to work in College Station on Good Friday through a miasma of dogwood and redbud and not feeling good about it at all. It was a sparkling, resplendent day. Thickets of wild plum threw up their dark arms in dreamy clouds of white. Primroses, tenderly pink and gold, filled up the ditches along the road.

I was not pleased. This was not a penitential landscape. Good Friday is not the time for beauty.

Yet here I was on my way to teach a bunch of nineteen-year-olds—most of whose minds were undefended by dogma, half of whom probably had no idea what Good Friday was all about—a poem that told them they should have their socks knocked off by the ersatz cherry trees blooming all about them. They were probably a good deal more concerned at present with their own hormones than the beauties of the woodland ride. But was converting them from hedonists to aesthetes any improvement?

I drove along, vaguely offended by the fields of flowers in full cry and the hillsides spangled with Easter white. This is the week, I thought, the Savior of the world dies. This is the day when all that is good and true goes down to suffer death at the hands of the arrogant, those swollen with the pride of power. And what is the world doing? What is the earth, its own life threatened by those same enemies, doing? Did it care? Was it grieving? No. It was shouldering aside the clods and the husks of its dead self in order to break into life. This unseemly riot had been going on for at least five days, in fact, ever since Palm Sunday—a term that sounded almost pagan itself. Another tree, another symbol of life had been flaunted in the face of suffering and death on that day, too.

As I watched the land roll by, it was as though this week, this so-called holy week, and this day, this tragically good Friday, were being mocked by the triumph of a fickle and unregarding life—life heedlessly, ruthlessly springing forth with relish, ignoring the torn placenta, the shriveling umbilical cord. Life ignoring the violated flesh and choked-off breath to which it owed its very existence, winking at the blood and muck from which it rose. Disregarding the cost.

I started up the range of hills that form the watershed of the Navasota River, glad to leave the flagrant fields behind me for a while. Dark pines rise up beside the highway there, shading out the understory trees and making vertical walls through which the road cuts toward Carlos, a community of itinerant coal miners who work in shifts for the regional power plant.

This was what Good Friday should be like, I thought. Somber and stripped. And here among the austere pines I could concentrate on what this day was about, could consider my own part in this necessary Good Friday.

All week I had been reading the penitential psalms and examining my sins. The exercise had been a satisfying one since my sins were clear and undeniable, and what was required of me to be rid of them was just as clear.

But now it was Good Friday. What did you do after you'd confessed all your sins and cleaned out all your closets? I took one last look around the bare cell of my heart for some forgotten fault, at the same time being careful to avoid the danger of manufacturing contrition for its own sake. Scruples, the small, sharp stones that score an overactive conscience, can also lead to the sin of self-indulgence, I knew.

But what else was there to do on Good Friday? Already, on this spring morning, as I was descending the hills toward the river, Jesus was beginning his climb to Golgotha. What else was there to do? For the women who followed him, "looking on afar off," for those standing beneath the cross, what was there left to do?

Nothing. Quite obviously just nothing. The soldier who confessed, "Truly this man was the Son of God," and the one who pierced his Savior's side with the spear, both were equally helpless there, I suddenly saw. Because Good Friday is the day when you can do nothing. Bewailing and lamenting your manifold sins does not in itself make up for them. Scouring your soul in a frenzy of spring cleaning only sterilizes it; it does not give it life. On Good Friday, finally, we are all, mourners and mockers alike, reduced to the same impotence. Someone else is doing the terrible work that gives life to the world. Good Friday is the day we can do nothing at all.

No matter that I repudiated my old transgressions. On Good Friday, all one's fine feelings count for nothing. If there was to be anything new about life after today, it had to come from some source beyond myself. That is why there was nothing more to do on Good Friday. *Our hope is built on nothing less than Jesus' blood and righteousness.* His blood and his righteousness.

I passed the intersection at Carlos with its one blinking, yellow light and crossed the bridge over the pipeline that carries the coal slurry to the plant a few miles further on. From there the road bent northward to cross the river.

As I broke out of the pines and into the fertile bot-

126

tomland, the spring again assaulted me. The land below, emerging from the tendrils of morning fog, was a tangle of luxuriant fertility. Clouds of pink and white, effulgent enough to inebriate the soberest soul, lured one's line of vision into the darker trees. Acres of bluebonnets streaked up the red clay banks of the river. The earth, on this Good Friday, cast forth its life, heedless of the sacrifice that sustained it. Its callous, regardless life, sucked from the source it can never repay, never replenish. Continually drawing on the death of its Savior to live. Just like me.

HOLY SATURDAY

——◆——

Eugene H. Peterson

Prettyfeather placed two buffalo-head nickels on the countertop for her Holy Saturday purchase: smoked ham hocks; two for a nickel. In the descending hierarchy of Holy Saturday foods, ham hocks were at the bottom.

Large hickory-smoked hams held center position in the displays in my father's butcher shop. Colorful cardboard cutouts provided by salesmen from the meat-packing companies of Armour, Hormel, and Silverbow all showed variations on a theme: a father at an Easter Sunday dinner table carving a ham, surrounded by an approving wife and scrubbed, expectant children.

Off to the side of these displays were stacks of the smaller and cheaper picnic hams (though a picnic ham is not, properly speaking, a ham at all, but the shoulder of the pig). There were no company-supplied pictures, nor even brand names on them. On Holy Saturday customers crowded into our store, responding to the sale signs painted on the plate-glass windows fronting Main Street and sorting themselves into upper and lower socio-economic strata: the affluent buying honey-cured, hickory-smoked hams, and the less-than-affluent buying unadjectived picnics.

Prettyfeather was the only person I ever remember buying ham hocks—gristly on the inside and leathery on the outside, but *smoked* and therefore emanating the aroma of a feast—on Holy Saturday. She was the only Indian I knew by name in the years of my childhood and youth, although I grew up in Indian country. Every Saturday she came into our store to make a small purchase: pickled pig's feet, chitlins, blood sausage, head cheese, pork liver.

She was always by herself. She wore moccasins and was wrapped in a blanket, even in the warmest weather. The coins she used for her purchases were in a leather pouch that hung like a goiter at her neck. Her face was the color and texture of the moccasins on her feet.

Indian was a near-mythological word for me, full of nobility and beauty, filled out with stories of the hunt and sacred ceremony. Somehow it never occurred to me that this Indian squaw who came into our store every Saturday and bought barely edible meats belonged to that nobility.

While she made her purchases from us and did whatever other shopping she did on these Saturdays in town, her husband and seven or eight other Indian braves sat on apple boxes in the alley behind the Pastime Bar and passed a jug of

Thunderbird wine. Several jugs, actually. As I made back-door deliveries of steaks and hamburger to the restaurants along Main Street, I passed up and down the alley several times each Saturday and watched the empty jugs accumulate. Late in the evening, Bennie Odegaard, son of one of the bar owners and a little older than me, would pull the braves into his dad's pickup truck and drive them out south of town to their encampment along the Stillwater River and dump them out.

I don't know how Prettyfeather got back to that small cluster of tarpaper shacks and teepees. She walked, I guess. Carrying her small purchases. On Holy Saturday she carried four ham hocks.

I had never heard of any Saturday designated as holy. It was simply Saturday. If, once a year, precision was required, it was "the Saturday before Easter." It was one of the heaviest workdays of the year. Beginning early in the morning, I carried the great, fragrant hams shipped from Armour in Spokane, Hormel in Missoula, and Silverbow in Butte, and arranged them symmetrically in pyramids. We had advertised all week long. Saturday was the commercial climax to the week. Holiness was put on hold till Sunday. Saturday was for working hard and making money.

It was a day when the evidence of hard work and its consequence—money—became publicly apparent. The evidence was especially clear on that particular Saturday, when we sold hundreds of hams to deserving Christians, and four ham hocks to an Indian squaw and her pickup load of drunks.

The Saturday pinned between Good Friday and Easter was one of the high-energy workdays of the year, with no thought of holiness. I grew up in a religious home that believed devoutly in the saving benefits of the death of Jesus and the glorious life of resurrection. But between these two polar events of the faith, we worked a long and lucrative day.

I would have been very surprised, and somewhat unbelieving, to have known that in the very town in which I worked furiously all those unholy Saturdays, there were people besides the Indians who were not working at all, nor spending, but were remembering the despair of a world disappointed in its grandest hopes, entering into the emptiness of death by deliberately emptying the self of illusion and indulgence and self-importance. Keeping vigil for Easter. Watching for the dawn.

And some of them listening to this ancient Holy Saturday sermon from a preacher now unknown:

Something strange is happening on earth today, a great silence, and stillness. The whole earth keeps silence because the King is asleep. The earth trembled and is still because God has fallen asleep in the flesh and he has raised up all who have slept ever since the world began. God has died in the flesh and hell trembles with fear.

He has gone to search for our first parent, as for a lost sheep. Greatly desiring to visit those who live in darkness and in the shadow of death, he has gone to free from sorrow the captive Adam and Eve, he who is both God and the son of Eve. The Lord approached them bearing the cross, the weapon that had won him the victory. At the sight of him Adam, the first man he had created, struck his breast in terror and cried out to everyone: "My Lord be with you all." Christ answered him: "And with your spirit." He took him by the hand and

raised him up, saying: "Awake, O sleeper, and rise from the dead, and Christ will give you light."
    —*The reading for Holy Saturday in the Liturgy of the Hours*

As it turned out, I interpreted the meaning of the world and the people around me far more in terms of the hard working on Saturday than anything said or sung on Friday and Sunday. Whatever was told me in those years (and I have no reason to doubt that I heard truth), what I absorbed in my bones was a liturgical rhythm in which the week reached its climax in a human workday, the results of which were enjoyed on Easter.

Those assumptions provided the grid for a social interpretation of the world around me: Saturday was the day for hard work, or for displaying its results, namely, money. If someone appeared neither working nor spending on Saturday, there was something wrong, catastrophically wrong. The Indians attempting a hungover Easter feast on ham hocks were the most prominent exhibit.

It was a view of life shaped by "The Gospel According to America." The rewards were obvious, and I enjoyed them. I still do. Hard work pays off. I learned much in those years that I will never relinquish.

Yet, there was one large omission that set all other truth dangerously at risk: the omission of holy rest. The refusal to be silent. The obsessive avoidance of emptiness. The denial of any experience and any people in the least bit suggestive of godforsakenness.

It was far more than an annual ignorance on Holy Saturday; it was religiously fueled, weekly arrogance. Not only was the Good Friday Crucifixion bridged to the Easter Resurrection by this day furious with energy and lucrative with reward, but all the gospel truths were likewise set as either introductions or conclusions to the human action that displayed our prowess and our virtue every week of the year. God was background to our business. Every gospel truth was maintained intact and all the human energy was wholly admirable, but the rhythms were all wrong, the proportions wildly skewed. Desolation—and with it companionship with the desolate, from first-century Semites to twentieth-century Indians—was all but wiped from consciousness.

But there came a point at which I was convinced that it was critically important to pay more attention to what God does than what I do; to find daily, weekly, yearly rhythms that would get that awareness into my bones. Holy Saturday for a start. And then, times to visit people in despair, and learn their names, and wait for resurrection.

Embedded in my memory now is this most poignant irony: those seven or eight Indians, with the Thunderbird empties lying around, drunk in the alley behind the Pastime Bar on Saturday afternoon, while we Scandinavian Christians worked diligently late into the night, oblivious to the holiness of the day. The Indians were in despair, *religious* despair, something very much like the Holy Saturday despair narrated in the Gospels. Their way of life had come to nothing, the only buffalo left to them engraved on nickels, a couple of which one of their squaws had paid out that morning for four bony ham hocks. The early sacredness of their lives was a wasteland; and they, godforsaken as they supposed, drugged their despair with Thunderbird and buried their dead visions and dreams in the alley behind the Pastime, ignorant of the God at work beneath their emptiness.

EASTER SUNDAY

Philip Yancey

My earliest memories from childhood have in common a single, overwhelming quality: fear.

I was not yet four when I awoke in the middle of the night to a wild pummeling at the door. Mother, in her bathrobe, unfastened the chain to let in a hysterical woman, then slammed and locked the door just in time. The woman's drunken husband was chasing her with a jagged, broken bottle.

For the next half-hour I lay in bed and listened to the sounds: inside, the woman's blubbery sobs; outside, the man's loud threats punctuated by the blows of his fist on our door and the shatter of glass from a bottle hurled against our brick wall. Then policemen came, and the light from their squad car swept across our apartment, eerily lighting in red the faces of neighbors who had gathered just outside.

Another memory: my mother's stern, mysterious warnings against a "nasty, nasty man" who had been seen in the neighborhood offering candy to little boys and girls. "Don't you *ever* go near him," she said, gripping my arm as if I already had. "Don't ever go beyond the swing set in the backyard."

The polio epidemic of 1950 had widowed my mother at the age of 26, and only now, as an adult looking back, can I sense the hardship she bore trying to rear two sons in a grim "white trash" housing project near Atlanta.

When I was five, we left that project for the country town of Ellenwood, a move that crossed a psychic distance from Charles Dickens to Mark Twain. We now lived on a divided dirt road, with a colonnade of trees running down its center, in a house that was connected to no one else's. My memories of that year come back in happy waves. The freight train that derailed, spilling mountains of bright green watermelons for us kids to climb, slide bumpily down, then lob at each other. The mule next door who gratefully ate all the too-large and too-bitter cucumbers from our garden. My mongrel dog, Buster Brown, who disgraced himself by wandering too close to an open septic tank. (No amount of raw meat would lure him up a slanted board, and we despaired of Buster's fate until a neighbor man, genuinely heroic, waded in to rescue him.)

In that house I first learned to ride a bike, and to read, and catch a baseball, and climb a tree, and swing out over a creek on a rope. And it was there one Easter Sunday that I learned the meaning of one of the most terrible words in the English language.

As far back as I can remember, we had a dog. They were all mixed breeds from the dog pound, and since we couldn't afford distemper shots they rarely lived long. But as soon as one died, another puppy would come along to chase away our grief. They marked my progression through childhood: "Oh, that's the year we had Rebel, just after Blackie died."

We never had cats, though, not until we moved to Ellenwood. An aunt in Philadelphia had let cats, scores of them, run wild in her row house, and there my mother had acquired a deep aversion. But finally, our first year in Ellenwood, Mother relented. We got a six-week-old kitten, solid black except for white "boots" on each of her legs—as if she had daintily stepped in a shallow dish of paint. Could she have any name but Boots?

Never was so much loving attention devoted to a kitten. My brother and I resolved to raise a pet so unblemished that our mother would desire a houseful of such sublime creatures. Boots lived in a cardboard box on the screened porch and slept on a pillow stuffed with cedar shavings. Forbidden to bring her inside the house, we spent most waking hours on that porch. Mother insisted that Boots must learn to defend herself before venturing into the huge outdoors, fixing a firm date of Easter Sunday for the kitten's first foray.

The final days before Easter tried our patience and fanned our longing. At long last the time arrived, the day of Boot's emergence.

The Georgia sun had already coaxed spring into full bloom. Easter morning began with the obligatory church service, after which we were required to line up like prisoners beside the tulips and daffodils for family pictures. I endured the picture-taking with much squinting and complaining, then yanked off my tie and ran to liberate Boots.

She sniffed her first blade of grass that day, and batted at her first daffodil, and stalked her first butterfly, leaping high in the air and missing. She kept us exuberantly entertained until neighbor kids descended upon us for a prearranged Easter egg hunt.

But when our next-door playmates arrived, the unthinkable happened. Their pet Boston terrier, Pugs, following them into our yard, spied Boots, let out one growl, and charged. I screamed, and we all ran toward Boots. But already Pugs had the tiny kitten in her mouth and was shaking it like a sock. We kids stood in a circle around the scene of violence, shrieking and making threatening motions to scare Pugs off. Helpless, we watched a whirl of flashing teeth and flying tufts of fur. Finally, Pugs dropped the kitten on the grass and trotted off, nonchalantly.

Boots had not yet died. She was mewing softly, and her eyes held a look of terror. Blood oozed from many puncture wounds, and her shiny black coat was flecked with Pugs's saliva. I prayed desperately that she would survive, and we all begged our parents to rush her to a veterinarian. But a neighbor pointed to the odd way Boots's head was jerked sideways. "Broken neck," he pronounced. "She'll never make it."

The adults shooed us away, and for many years we did not learn what happened next: they placed Boots in a burlap bag and held her under water in the creek, putting her out of her misery.

I could not have articulated it at the time, but what I

learned that Easter under the noonday sun was the ugly word *irreversible.* All afternoon I prayed for a miracle. *No! It can't be! Tell me it's not true!* Maybe Boots wouldn't really die. Or maybe she would die but come back—hadn't the Sunday-school teacher told such a story about Jesus?

Or maybe the whole morning could somehow be erased, rewound, and played over again minus that horrid scene. We could keep Boots on the screened porch forever, never allowing her outside. Or we could talk our neighbors into building a fence for Pugs. A thousand schemes ran through my mind over the next days, until the reality finally won over, and I accepted at last that Boots was dead. Irreversibly dead.

From then on, Easter Sundays in my childhood were stained by the memory of violence and death in the grass. And as the years increased I learned much more about the word *irreversible.* Once in the woods a friend and I lined up seventeen box turtles beside the creek and proceeded to drop heavy boulders on them, laughing as their shells cracked and their insides spurted out. That act of cruelty, my own cruelty, shocked me beyond measure. It defied my deep love of animals, and I long lived under its shadow of shame and guilt. I yearned for some way to erase it, to reverse it.

There followed a whole succession of scenes I likewise wished to reverse: fights with bullies, broken arms, foolish comments in class, unexpected pop quizzes, the inevitable first automobile accident, and all the other minor jolts of growing up, each one underscoring the dreadful word *irreversible.*

I had not escaped tragedy by moving from the housing project to an idyllic setting on a country lane; I had merely changed the setting where my life, both tragic and joyful, would play itself out. Life is like that for adults as well, I was to learn. We never quite grow used to it, but we concede that life consists of moments of joy and sadness all tossed together in a crazy salad. Over time, the tragedies may wear us down so that we no longer fight them. We grow conditioned to the irreversible.

After years of urban living had ground down my childhood love of nature, I found it suddenly rekindled through my friendship with a young photographer named Bob McQuilkin. I was working as a magazine editor at the time, and Bob seemed determined to drag me out of my stale routine and reintroduce me to the joyous world outside.

Once Bob drove his jeep to my office and insisted that I come see two baby owls he'd just rescued. For months he fussed over those scraggly orphaned owls, chasing barn mice and lizards to feed them, then trying to teach them to hunt on their own and to fly. (Bob teaching a bird to fly!) They'd flutter in soaking wet from a rainstorm—not wise enough yet to find shelter—and Bob would patiently pull out his electric hair dryer and blow them dry.

Two baby raccoons visited Bob's house every few days. (And why not? He would fix them an exotic crabmeat omelette.) On warm summer evenings, he opened the skylight above his bed and an obliging bat named Radar would swoop in with free mosquito-extermination services. You simply could not escape reminders of the natural world in Bob's home—he had built an aquarium into the side of the bathroom wall.

Bob was as fully "alive" as anyone I have ever known. And so when I heard this past October that Bob had died on a scuba-diving assignment in Lake Michigan, I could hardly absorb the news. Bob, dead? It was inconceivable. I could picture Bob doing anything at all—anything but lying still. But that is my last image of him: a thirty-six-year-old body in a blue-plaid flannel shirt lying in a casket. The old, ugly word *irreversible* came flooding back. I would never ski with Bob again, never sit with him for hours viewing slides, never again eat rattlesnake meat or buffalo burgers at his house.

Susan, his widow, asked me to speak at Bob's memorial service. Without a doubt, it was the hardest thing I have ever done. When I stood before them, the magazine editors and art directors and family and neighbors and friends, they reminded me of little birds—Bob's owls—with their mouths open begging for food. Begging for words of solace, for hope. What could I offer them?

I began by telling them what I had been doing the very afternoon Bob was making his last dive. That Wednesday I was sitting, oblivious, in a café at the University of Chicago, reading *The Quest for Beauty*, by Rollo May. In that book the famous therapist recalls scenes from his lifelong search for beauty, among them a visit to Mount Athos, a Greek peninsula on which there are a number of monasteries.

One morning, Rollo May happened to stumble upon the celebration of Greek Orthodox Easter, the tail end of a church service that had been proceeding all night long. Incense hung in the air. The only light came from candles. And at the height of that service, the priest gave everyone present three Easter eggs, wonderfully decorated and wrapped in a veil. "*Christos Anesti!*" he said—"Christ is risen!" Each person there, including Rollo May, responded according to custom, "He is risen indeed!"

Rollo May writes, "I was seized then by a moment of

spiritual reality: what would it mean for our world if He had truly risen?"

I read Rollo May's question the afternoon that Bob died, and it kept floating around in my mind, hauntingly, after I heard the news. What did it mean for our world that Christ had risen? Why were monks staying up all night to celebrate it? The early Christians had staked everything on the Resurrection, so much so that the apostle Paul wrote in 1 Corinthians, "And if Christ has not been raised, our preaching is useless and so is your faith" (15:14, NIV).

In the cloud of grief over Bob's death, I began to see the meaning of Easter in a new light. As a five-year-old on Easter Sunday I had learned the harsh lesson of irreversibility. Ironically, now as an adult I saw that Easter actually offered an awesome promise of *reversibility*. Nothing—no act of childhood cruelty, no experience of shame or remorse, and, no, not even death—was final. Even that could be reversed.

On Friday Jesus' closest friends had let the relentless crush of history snuff out all their dreams. Two days later, when the crazy rumors about Jesus' missing body shot through Jerusalem, they couldn't dare to believe. They were too conditioned to the irreversible. Only personal appearances by Jesus convinced them that something new, absolutely new, had broken out on earth. When that sank in, those same men who had slunk away in fear at Calvary were soon preaching to large crowds in the streets of Jerusalem.

At Bob McQuilkin's funeral, I rephrased Rollo May's question in the terms of our own grief. What would it mean for us if Bob rose again? We were sitting in a chapel, numbed by three days of grief and sadness, the weight of death bearing down upon us. What would it be like to walk outside to the parking lot and there, to our utter astonishment, find Bob.

Bob! With his bounding walk, his crooked grin, and clear gray eyes.

That image gave me a hint of what Jesus' disciples felt on the first Easter. They, too, had grieved for three days. But on Sunday they caught a glimpse of something else, a startling clue to the riddle of the universe. Easter hits a new note, a note of hope and faith that what God did once in a graveyard in Jerusalem, he can and will repeat on a grand scale, for the world. For Bob. For us. Against all odds, the irreversible can be reversed.

The German theologian Jürgen Moltmann expresses in a single sentence the great span from Good Friday to Easter. It is, in fact, a summary of human history, past, present, and future: "God weeps with us so that we may someday laugh with him."

ASCENSION

❦

Gregory Wolfe

Love is most nearly itself
When here and now cease to matter.
—T. S. ELIOT

When I first visited my sister at the state hospital, I wasn't fully prepared for the experience. As my mother drove the car through the front gates, the grounds of the hospital had the appearance of a rather exclusive liberal arts college. A long, tree-lined drive eventually gave way to the center of the "campus," where a number of stately brick buildings were clustered together. There were also a couple of handsome houses on the property, one of which would have been suitable for the president's mansion. I wouldn't have been surprised to see undergraduates strolling about, carrying books, sipping soft drinks, and tossing Frisbees.

But there were no college students; the grounds of the hospital were devoid of people. There wasn't even the normal bustle of coming and going that one associates with most hospitals. The quiet was unnerving.

As we entered the building where my sister was staying, no receptionist was present to greet us. The vestibule was small: no furniture, a worn linoleum floor littered with cigarette butts, a narrow doorway leading to a dirty toilet, and the main door into the hospital. This main door, of heavy steel and glass construction, was locked.

My mother picked up a wall phone, punched three numbers, and spoke rapidly into it. Her actions were brisk, habitual. She had done this many times before. In about three minutes, the door opened and one of the hospital staff silently led us through and into an elevator that took us to the third floor.

When we emerged from the elevator, the silence ended abruptly. The noise wasn't deafening, but it was manifold. It took me some time to process this strange diversity of sounds and break it down into its elements. I heard strident, raucous laughter; prolonged coughing fits; furious shouting; grouchy mutterings—all glued together by the constant drone of a television.

I should have known what to expect of a hospital for the mentally ill. But the contrast between the peace and order outside and the anarchy inside was too radical. All of the stereotypes and clichés that I had carried about in my mental baggage for years and years came streaming out. This is the place, I thought, which I had casually thought of as the insane asylum, the looney bin, the nuthouse. This is where people claim to be God or Jesus or Napoleon, where bug-eyed Jack Nicholson look-alikes smash people over the head with hammers.

Like so many people who have not confronted the phenomenon directly, I tended to associate mental illness with the grotesque and the freakish. What I felt in the hospital was not loathing or contempt but panic, helplessness, and the need to escape. Even the relatively straightforward case of mental retardation causes me to feel deep discomfort. Grief, pity, and powerlessness combine and make me seize up. This is beyond me, I think. I am inadequate. It isn't a lack of compassion but an inability to see how compassion can deal with so intractable a problem.

And yet, there I was: not a detached observer but a brother coming to visit his sister. Love for my own flesh and blood, my only sibling, struggled with my instinctive desire to escape from this kind of problem.

My sister, K., had been in and out of hospitals and halfway houses in New York, California, and New England for several years before my first visit to that mental hospital. She had also spent periods of time on the streets—with punk rockers in Greenwich Village and with lowlifes in Los Angeles. My parents spared no effort in trying to get K. the best care available. The number of hours they spent on K.'s behalf—on the phone, in the car, exploring treatment options—were beyond calculation. But K. inevitably sabotaged any new and promising program, usually by screaming obscenities and insults. No halfway house would keep her. She couldn't handle the idea of facing increased responsibility and independence.

145

The time came when K. was in too much danger to allow her out on her own. Sex, drugs, and alcohol were destroying her body and intensifying the symptoms of her mental illness. The last resort had been reached: K. had to be legally committed to a mental institution.

Ultimately, it became clear that K.'s tendency to dice with death was a form of self-abuse. At the center of her illness is an utter lack of self-esteem, a sense of worthlessness and despair that hangs on her soul like a millstone.

K. has taken this desire to mutilate herself to a very literal extreme. Her forearms are dotted with white, lumpy circles of scar tissue, the result of pressing the lighted end of a cigarette into her flesh. Here, too, I find the limits of my emotional balance; I cannot look at these scars, these stigmata of K.'s suffering.

I learned most of this from my parents, over the telephone. Since leaving home for college in the Midwest, graduate studies in England, and work in various places, I have seen K. only two or three days each year. Now that she has been committed, I see her at the hospital, or for brief outings, when her behavior warrants a pass.

When the two of us spend an afternoon together we do simple things: we go to a movie or wander about a shopping mall. Deprived of so many normal pleasures, K. has developed a passion for junk food. She also wants me to treat her to these goodies; they become the small sacraments that betoken my love for her. I buy her cigarettes, cheeseburgers, popcorn, beef jerky, coffee, donuts, bubble gum.

On these excursions we spontaneously return to the one thing we hold in common: our childhood. We become kids again—teasing, joking, pigging out. Whatever may come between us, whatever scar tissue accumulates on our bodies and our souls, nothing can take our childhood away.

As I sat in the cramped meeting room on that first visit to the hospital, I knew that K. was *not* a freak or a lunatic. The cheerful, tough, appealing girl that I knew as a child still shines through from time to time. The schizophrenia that debilitates her, scrambles her thoughts and her words, leads her up to manic heights and down to depressive depths, cannot utterly efface the stamp of her personality. There are times when I look at K., knowing of her pathetic and dangerous episodes with sex and drugs in previous years, and am overwhelmed by the feeling that her inmost being is still, somehow, innocent.

The hardest thing about visiting K.—harder than her occasional bursts of hate and mockery—is leaving her. Our times together are so few that I cannot help feeling guilty about the long gaps of time that lie between the visits. Each time I leave her at the door of her hospital building, a door that locks behind her, I drive back to my wife and children, to my own busy career and accomplishments, to the relative order of a domestic and professional life that she may never know.

I am her big brother, whom she always looked up to. Her constant refrain in childhood still sounds in my memory. "Right, Greg?" she would say, turning to me for validation and support. Now she must feel that there is a dark, unbridgeable abyss between us. From her psychic inferno she sees me return to what must seem to her an unimaginable paradise.

Psychiatrists and counselors tell me that I have to forgive myself and recognize my own needs and responsibilities. There is truth in this, and yet each parting seems a betrayal.

For someone in K.'s condition, long-distance love is insufficient. Sending her gifts is problematic: she tends to give away the few things that are not stolen from her. The telephone is too abstract. And K. doesn't have an attention span that will last out a letter of more than a few paragraphs.

As I drive out of the hospital grounds and back into the world, a host of questions press themselves on me. When I am away, does she continue to feel that I love her and need her love? Will she forgive, and understand, my awkwardness and self-consciousness? Will I think of her, and pray for her, as often as I should? And then there is the ineluctable question, addressed to K.'s Creator: Why, dear God, should this child of yours have a clouded mind and white scars on her arms?

I know now that I may never have answers to these questions. At first I tried to cope with the irrationality of K.'s condition by turning to theology for rational answers. But it soon became obvious that theological terms alone could not bridge the gap between my head and my heart.

It is only when I let go of the restless, analytical part of my mind that I have moved closer to an inward reconciliation about my relationship with K. For me, this has meant prayer, and meditation on the Gospels. In placing my own story alongside that of Christ, I have discovered analogies and resonances that tell me more than any intellectual abstractions could ever do.

It was in praying the rosary, an old Catholic form of meditative prayer which focuses on the key events in the life of Christ, that I recognized a parallel to my agonized separations from K: the Ascension.

The Ascension is one of the most difficult scenes to recreate in the imagination. The temptation for most of us, I suspect, is to accept one of the visual clichés that come down

to us, to picture the Ascension as if it were the finale of some
florid Italian opera, with Jesus lifting off the ground into a
shining firmament to the accompaniment of massed choirs.

I prefer to focus on the human dimension of the disciples'
experience, rather than give in to this grandiose but remote
version of the Ascension. I have found myself wondering
what the disciples felt as they witnessed the Lord departing
from them.

Try as I might, I cannot believe that the disciples felt
joyful and triumphant at this moment. It seems to me more
likely that their hearts were stirring with a mixture of confusion, awe, sorrow, and hope. Both at the empty tomb and at
the Ascension, the disciples needed an angel to break the
trance of their disbelief and incomprehension and direct them
to a truth beyond their imagining. "Why are you men from
Galilee standing here looking into the sky? Jesus who has
been taken up from you into heaven, this same Jesus will
come back in the same way as you have seen him go there"
(Acts 1:11).

What must it have been like in those first moments when
the disciples realized that he was gone from among them? The
sense of loss, even of desolation, must have been palpable.

It seems to me that Jesus, in his humanity, also felt the
pain of separation. A note of sadness permeates the many
prophecies of the Passion he made to the disciples. There is
the awful loneliness of Gethsemane, and the sense of abandonment on the cross. And it is from the cross that he gives John
to Mary as a substitute son.

In the forty days after the Resurrection, the disciples had
begun to learn that he would no longer be accessible to them
as he had been. The risen Lord appeared among them suddenly, only to vanish abruptly. At times he was unrecogniz-

able. This was to be the new mode. Having fulfilled his mission, he would henceforth be caught only in glimpses, some of which we would not even recognize at first.

We begin to understand that Jesus was teaching the disciples—and all of us—that we must discover him in the circumstances of our own lives, learn to discern his presence. But this is a hard lesson for most of us to master. When, in the midst of suffering, God's presence and will are elusive, it is difficult not to feel that he has ascended beyond our reach.

At times such as these, it is as if we were stuck between Ascension and Pentecost. We have experienced love, success, moments of vision, a happy childhood or marriage, but now they are gone. When, if ever, will they return?

Jesus felt the anguish of separation; but paradoxically he also taught the hard lesson that it would lead to a higher and more satisfying union. He entrusted his mother to the care of his beloved disciple, yet he denied her relationship to him. "Who are my mother and my brothers? Anyone who does the will of God, that person is my brother and mother" (Mark 3:33, 35). A man and a woman leave their families to cling to each other in marriage; their union will create another family and expand the circle of love. The grain of wheat must fall off the stalk and down to the ground if it is to achieve new life.

Like Doubting Thomas, we crave physical contact—the here and now—to assure us of the reality of love. There is something intensely human about this need. I want to be with my sister to demonstrate my love for her, to make sure she feels it.

But love only becomes complete when it is not dependent on time and place. T. S. Eliot, probably the greatest Christian poet of the twentieth century, wrote: "Love is most

150

nearly itself/When here and now cease to matter." Love makes the beloved present; it collapses dimensions. Love does not eradicate pain and suffering; it enfolds them in a higher synthesis.

"I am going away, and shall return," Jesus told the disciples in his farewell discourse (John 14:28). The disciples—an intensely human group indeed—must have felt both anxiety and comfort at these words. But it had to be. Of the Ascension, Romano Guardini, in his superb life of Christ, *The Lord*, wrote, "So Jesus left—only in the same instant to return in a new form. He entered eternity, into an existence that is entirely love. . . . Ever since, Christ's manner of being has been that of love. Hence, because he loves us . . . his going away into the fulfillment of love really means that he is 'with us' more fully than ever before."

I know that my sister, K., though subject to mood swings and bouts of depression, still looks up to her big brother. I believe that, deep in her heart, she wants me to go off and do what I have been called to do in life. I can only hope that in her loneliness and pain she understands that my love for her is unconditional.

Jesus opened the gates of heaven for us. Pentecost, his return into our hearts, gives each of us the foretaste of perfect union. The universal language of his love speaks plainly to our divided world. In heaven there will be no more tears, no more separations, and all scars will be healed.

PENTECOST

~

Calvin Miller

Pentecost 1966 found me in Brussels in the Cathedral of St. Michael. The holiday mass offered me an hour of reflection as the high worship flew at me in two languages: Latin, which I understood only intermittently, and Flemish, which I understood not at all. Thirty of us had gathered in the great cathedral, which stretched cavernous and dark behind us.

The Eucharist was most medieval and colorful. The office was read by a red-robed cardinal attended by two Swiss guards. The great church seemed to embarrass the little crowd, huddled at the altar end of the cathedral, with all its officious gallantry and plumage of the worship leader. The ghostly echoes of the holy words flew through the vacuous and dank air of the middle earth stones.

I fashioned the unintelligible service to be about the Holy Spirit, so I thumbed my English Bible to Acts 2 and tried to keep faith with the cardinal, who was totally unaware that a Baptist from America was there, spying on his litany but very much in need of a word from the Lord.

No matter! It was Pentecost: a day for celebrating that time when power once fell upon the church; the wind blew then, the flame danced, too. Indeed, the miter of the bishop was in the shape of flame to recall the descent of the warm, indwelling God of Whitsunday. The infilling, overarching near-end of the Trinity came slashing across the language barriers to reveal himself to me.

The bishop swung the censer, and the odor of incense drifted from the altar, heady as new wine. I suddenly understood why the early churches were accused of a giddy and immoderate inebriation. Drunk on God were those the Spirit washed. They were elated, out of touch with their business-for-business, commerce-controlled world. They danced the streets mad with joy, speaking in languages they'd never learned, to foreigners from countries they'd never visited. Thus Pentecost was born in this *mysterium tremendum*.

Acts 2 swam my reverie, calling to mind a rustic Oklahoma tent revival, where I first met the Holy Spirit two decades earlier. I was nine years old in that important year when World War II ended. Hiroshima and Nagasaki each sounded a little like American Indian tribes and each had the same number of syllables and sounds as Oklahoma. I couldn't imagine exactly where they were, but the whole world had come to focus on their desperation. The adults in my world talked of little else. The pictures, under headline letters thick as my young fingers, covered the newspapers black with smudgeable ink. My four older brothers-in-law would come home, they said. Indeed, we thanked God that the possibility of their dying had passed.

In that very year of joy and cataclysm, the Pentecostals erected a tent. There was very little use in asking where Pentecostals got tents. It was like asking where Ringling Brothers got tents. Pentecostals had tents, that's all! And they came to *our* town. Their big-top tabernacle rose above a swampy, snakey lot and was wind-billowed like the happy accordions that filled the canvas like sails. The tent swayed but never fell, for it was held upward by staked ropes, taut as the guitar strings that played along with the reedy accordions. The tent looked like a huge orange jack-o'-lantern, lit by dangling light bulbs, around which swarmed the candleflies of August. Revivals always came with August, as medicine shows came with June. Both peddled their wares in these canvas cathedrals, floored with wood chips, domed with tarpaulins, and pewed with 2 × 12's resting on concrete blocks.

Here I, too, found myself, seated on the boards, shirtless (you could get by with that in 1945 if you were a child), shoeless ("no shoes, no shirt, no service" was sloganized by restaurants, not Pentecostals). Worst of all, I was not "saved." Oklahoma Pentecostals had divided all the world into two broad categories: saved and unsaved. By the age of nine or so most everyone secretly knew which category was theirs. Indeed, that's why we had tent revivals, so people could change categories.

The person who helped with the changing of the categories was the Holy Spirit. That was what the Spirit did. He helped the lost get saved, and the saved act more like it. Most of the *dramatis personae* of this rural drama now escape me. I do remember two huge Gepettos who played monstrous "John Deere" accordions. There was also an unforgettable reformed drunkard who, through streaming tears, told how he had once been set free of the devil's power. One of the athletic evangelists wore a leather buckskin coat, whose swishing, dangling strips of cowhide fringe lured the eye hypnotically as he made the earth tremble with his gargantuan glossolalia.

I listened, sincerely and with fear. Who wouldn't? As Nagasaki yet smoldered, this red-eyed prophet told us of the great whore in Rome who would fornicate with the antichrist till blood flowed to the horses' bridles. I trembled as he warned us to make ready for apocalyptic hordes of frogs and locusts. The Euphrates would be dry as the Salt Fork (a sun-dried river of northern Oklahoma), he said, then Gog and Magog would rise up and the real tribulation would begin to tribulate. I quailed wide-eyed as the buckskin jacket rippled on the chest of this doomsdayer who spoke with authority and not as the liberal Methodists and Presbyterians did.

This matter was serious. The hymns made me as nervous as the preaching, for they were rapturously exultant about death and all the great things that would come once we had all had the good fortune to die. "Some glad morning when this life is o'er, we'll fly away," said one hymn. Another rhapsodized, "Almost cannot avail, almost is but to fail, sad sad the bitter wail, almost but lost." But the song that choked my voice to silence went, "I was sinking deep in sin, far from the peaceful shore, very deeply stained within, sinking to rise no more." Oh, the pain I felt as the accordions lamented my childhood fate. I saw only "the dark wave," oh how I needed "the lifeline to be saved."

"*In nomine Patri, et Filii, et Spiritus Sancti*"; the cardinal chanted the thread that bound the mass in Brussels to my aimless mental crossing of my childhood years. While his Latin office rolled by, I wondered if the cardinal knew "Farther Along" and "I'll Fly Away." His red robe fascinated me and so did the medieval garb of Beefeaters, who stood like altar guards staring into the long, dark cavern of St. Michael's. The cardinal's robe swished as he pivoted and latinated. Suddenly I realized how different his dress was from the buckskins of the evangelist who preached in the Pentecostal tent. "We all have our own denominational costumes," I thought. Suddenly he lifted the cup, genuflected, and spoke again of the Spiritus Sanctus. Somehow I knew we were brothers. He convinced me he was "saved."

I'm not sure he would have convinced the evangelist or Sister Rose, our Pentecostal pastor. She, too, was at the revival that Shekinah night when Nagasaki burned in my heart. She, too, knew the Spirit, I could tell. Sister Rose didn't play around at being religious. She clamped her eyes shut and lifted her head as though she could see through both her clenched eyelids and the canvas that domed our primitive glory. "Shandala," she glossolalized. Tears streamed down her face. Sister Rose was truly "filled" (with the Holy Ghost). Even Sister Rodgers said so, and Sister Rodgers had the gift of discernment, which meant she, more than others, could tell who was truly filled and who wasn't.

I wasn't. Sister Rodgers would know that too, of course. So when they began to sing "Oh Why Not Tonight?" it seemed an honest question unblemished by the adenoidal alto harmony that always marked our singing of the invitation. "Step forward to the altar, so you'll never have to step into hell," shouted the buckskinned evangelist above the plaintive singing. Sister Rose was weeping. Sister Rodgers was discerning. The burden was immense. I broke into tears. Emotion burned like fire through the sawdust chips.

Hell, dark as a gospel tent in a power outage, suddenly gaped like a black hole before me. I stood weeping, naked, foolish, and undone. What would I do if God should bring Gog to Garfield County? I knew not when Christ would come! Lucky for me, they sang an invitation: "Oh, do not let the Word depart, and close thine eyes against the light, poor sinner harden not your heart, be saved, oh, tonight."

I had no choice. I must fly now to the arms of Jesus. I did. Wonder of wonder, he did all the hymn said. He snatched my feet from the fiery clay and set me on the rock. I changed categories. I was saved.

The woodchip aisle was a kind of yellow brick road that ended in Oz. I was saved, said Sister Rose, but Sister Rodgers said I was truly filled. They were both right, of course, said Brother Buckskin, and I felt a marvelous elation. I then knew what the Bible was saying to me in the Brussels cathedral.

And when the day of Pentecost was fully come, they were all with one accord in one place. And suddenly there came a sound from heaven as of a rushing mighty wind, and it filled all the house where they were sitting. And there appeared unto them cloven tongues like as of fire, and it sat upon each of them. And they were all filled with the Holy Ghost, and began to speak with other tongues, as the Spirit gave them utterance. . . . Others mocking said, These men are full of new wine.

But Peter, standing up with the eleven, lifted up his voice, and said unto them, Ye men of Judea, and all ye that dwell in Jerusalem, be this known unto you, and

hearken to my words: For these are not drunken, as ye
suppose, seeing it is but the third hour of the day. But
this is that which was spoken by the prophet Joel; And
it shall come to pass in the last days, saith God, I will
pour out of my Spirit upon all flesh: and your sons and
your daughters shall prophesy, and your young men
shall see visions, and your old men shall dream dreams:
And on my servants and on my handmaidens I will pour
out in those days of my Spirit; and they shall prophesy:
And I will shew wonders in heaven above, and signs in
the earth beneath; blood, and fire, and vapour of smoke:
The sun shall be turned into darkness, and the moon
into blood, before that great and notable day of the Lord
come: And it shall come to pass, that whosoever shall
call on the name of the Lord shall be saved. (Acts
2:1–4, 13–21)

The cardinal did not seem nearly as moving as Sister
Rose once did. Still, I felt the years condense: 1945 and 1966
were one. That's what the Spirit does. He condenses, inte-
grates, and unifies all years and all saving experience. As a
matter of fact, Joel 2:28 binds the ages before Christ with
Peter's ecstatic sermon of AD 27, with Chrysostom, Augustine, Aquinas, and yes, Sister Rose. To be sure, all ages,
cultures, and churches go about it differently, but we are yet
made one by the *Spiritus Sanctus.*

Pentecost is not merely a day on the church calendar; it
is fire and wind able to blow and burn anytime. The elation
is inebriating. It comes suddenly like the wind of which Jesus
said, "The wind bloweth where it listeth, and thou hearest
the sound thereof, but canst not tell whence it cometh, and
whither it goeth: so is every one that is born of the Spirit"

(John 3:8). And, like the Jerusalem pilgrims, our elation must make us appear as though we have gotten "drunk on God" (Acts 2:13ff) and the joy binds the ages. Jesus, in the John passage on the Spirit, speaks of being born again (John 3:3). The Acts passage on the Spirit ends with a mass conversion of pilgrims. Conversion is always the first, best work of the Spirit of God.

In my life it was true. I wondered about the priest. How did he come to know the Spirit? How diverse must be the ways of God to make an educated cardinal and a bashful child of nine one in Christ. Still, this is his most glorious work, unitive across our wide church differences.

I have a distant friend who helped liberate Belsen in 1945. He said that as he leaned against a wall of execution, he looked out at the now silent concentration camp and saw the grim reminder of man's inhumanity. The greatness of the moment overcame him and the Spirit soared into his life. C. S. Lewis came more gradually to know the Spirit's reality. He wrangled on a bus top and in a motorcycle sidecar with the very existence of God his mind tried to deny! But, no matter, Spirit's coming is authentic in whatever manner it occurs.

But what of the cardinal? What of me? The coming of the Spirit in my life certainly lacks the historical grandeur of the liberation of Belsen. As a child, I merely knelt between big Pentecostal women in the sawdust, and there he came. But the experience is as indelible as "young men having visions, and old men dreaming dreams, and women preaching the glory of his coming" (Acts 2:17).

In my devotion, the cardinal all too abruptly swished away. The mass was over. In a way I felt cheated. The wafer and wine were not for me, a Protestant. Church doctrine can sometimes mar a beautiful experience, but while it might bar me from the table, the faith had been opened. I walked out of the dark church. The sun drenched the world with glorious sunlight which, like the Spirit, unified the world. The costumes were gone, the hookers who had been in the congregation were all back in the streets. Neon blinked its glitzy enticement from bistro to bistro.

Never mind!

There was a fire loose in the world that made Jerusalem, Oklahoma, and Belgium all one. It wasn't as obvious as I might have liked outside the cathedral. But the integrating Spirit was there . . . and would always be. Who knows where the wind may yet blow? Where the flame may yet surprise us? Such a fire is ever in us even when it hides, waiting to reveal itself where the coldness of reason freezes.

TRINITY SUNDAY

Karen Burton Mains

Something lost to me forty years ago has been found again. It is like a love letter, hidden in a drawer beneath the paper liner, which falls through a crack to the bureau floor, forgotten, only to be discovered by a delighted housewife, the fruit of her impulsive cleaning spree. It is like a garden trowel, hunted by the gardener in the garage, in the shed, only to appear after spring thaw, wedged in the soil of the perennial bed, right where it is needed. I have found this lost thing again, something precious to me when I was a little child growing up. It is the memory of a boy whose olive-hued skin, dark when pressed for comparison against my own small forearm, satisfied me. He was my first friend. We were a pleasing contrast, blond hair against brunette, blue eyes and brown. Before all others he was the first love.

I have been remembering this little boy these days and considering what I lost when I lost him. I lost a co-regency we shared over the wooden block world that sprawled on the playroom floor: circles and cylinders and rectangles and squares and triangles and half-moons, which became viaducts, and train tracks, cities, villages, roundabouts and towers. I lost my psychological twin, the male half of the female me mirrored in his child-self. I lost the innocence of play, that of boy and girl together. I lost the insouciance of the child-cry, "My friend! My friend!" Ever since, I have guarded the use of that word, used it for only one other male, my husband. Even so, he is often too busy to know how rarely this gift is given by me or how to treasure it. I have become wary about loving, closing my heart against a tenderness that makes me weak and vulnerable.

I found first love again in this my fifth decade. The memory was evoked because I have been tracking the Trinity. Like a hound yapping after scent, I hunt signs of the holy triad. Weary of the privatism of the Western church, appalled by solo salvationists, I want a trinitarianism that affects my living. The results of the chase have surprised me. Threes, threes and threes keep falling in my path; a triad here, its obverse imprint there, a clue in trilogies, lines in trimeter. Triumverates land willy-nilly. I cherish a copy of the icon *The Holy Trinity* by the Russian master, Rublev. The original hangs in the Tretiakov Gallery in Moscow. Three forms lean slightly, deferring to one another: God the Father, God the Son, and God the Holy Spirit. The grouping is configured upon a circle and conveys a harmonious equilibrium of composition—the soft colors of the robes, the symbols of the iconographic lexicon, light falling across the ancient faces.

In prayer, I often find myself pressing the picture against my forehead, or against my heart. Like blotter paper absorbing ink, my flesh soaks up sacramental peace from this visual image. At middle-age, I want Rublev's icon in reality. I am weary of breached fraternity. There are too many aborted friendships. I want to speak the word *brother* in all truth and not demean it by triteness. I am demanding union inwardly and unity outwardly.

The hunt has taken surprising turnings. I am amazed. For instance, I have found the growing memory of first love. Reconciliation litters the track behind me. I am learning to trust Man again. Nor did I know I had become so chary. At a meeting recently, I was reminded why. One of my male colleagues turned an angry visage and dumped upon me his rage. I had been defending another woman staff member against stern, inappropriate harshness. My advocacy offended my board colleague. The more he talked, the angrier he became, his face white and tightening. An inner warning signal flashed: A male/female issue! A male/female issue! Later, it was reported that this man had privately groused about "domineering females." Thud! The Punch and Judy show again, a variation in suburbia, a revival in this west end.

In my childhood, communion was always served by a regiment of male elders, marching intent down the aisles, proceeding in timed steps, with cold aluminum trays containing broken crackers and miniature glasses of grape juice. Sober-faced, hands folded above their belt buckles, they guarded us as we fed on the body and blood of Christ. And

I have been running into these stern and disapproving men ever since. The place to which they assigned me, a woman, I do not fit; indeed I am the proverbial misfit.

But I have been chasing Trinity. I am determined to name other men beside my husband as friends—one, a nuclear physicist, whose admirable fidelity allows me safe working collegiality. He has the uncanny ability to speak truth simply. I quietly moan, "One of the men on the board thinks I'm a domineering woman." My friend the physicist leans across our lunch table and says, "Then, whoever he is, this man, he doesn't know you." Of course. Of course—he doesn't know me. Instead of adding the angry colleague to my "watch-out" list, I am plotting reconciliation. I am blessing my enemy. Trinity demands my collaboration in reunity. Chasing further is impossible until I jab at restoration. Men can wound, women can wound; but women can also heal, men can be healers.

The memory of my lost first love came forcibly to mind one afternoon when my pastor stood at my door making polite overtures for departure. That week, life had ambushed me, and he tenderly brought to me gifts of Christian charity: prayer, the Scriptures, oil and communion. In the hallway, I stood on tiptoe to his height to brush his cheek with a good-bye, thank-you gesture. At that moment he bent to kiss my hand. We bumped foreheads, laughed suddenly, said farewell. Closing the door after him, I pressed the small of my back against the protruding knob. Car wheels crunched outside on the driveway gravel. Then I felt the tangible presence of peace, wing-brushes of the dove, soft upon my soul.

What is this, I wondered, this feeling of peace? From where does it come? I considered my just-departed pastor.

His inviolate covenant to the sacred ministrations of clergy/ priest has given me safety also. That I understand. But how had we developed a male/female relationship without rancor? How had we come to an absence of competition which ordinarily baits men and women to race each other breathless? No sexuality pushed or pulled between us. I felt comfort and sanctuary.

There was something familiar in this peace, something known once, long ago—a sound whistled in memory, from far off. What was it? I calculated all the other man/woman relationships in my life—moments in marriage so sweet, so unsophisticated that I have endured the passages of living widowhood caused by my husband's workaholism. The tallying of sums, both negative and positive, continued—boyfriends, male acquaintances, fathers, colleagues, professional peers. Back, back, I totalled, back to childhood, finally back to a little boy named Allen, back to my very first love.

His child face was now in mind, and the audio memo yielded a plethora of remembrances: laughter, a joyous gurgle from the back of a boy's gullet, rising, bumping up inside, across each rib (*ch* ah-hah, *ch* ah-*ch* ah-hah). Then, visual memory: skinny legs crisscrossed Indian style, two sweaty heads, one brunette and one with damp blond curls, bent unself-consciously close to examine bugs on the ground. My first-friend! My first-friend! Three or four years old we must have been, kindergartners together, then early grade-schoolers. And oh! our play—we jumped from impossible heights, from the courtyard gateposts into the plantain lily beds. In our garden dominion, we popped the purple blooms, tiny balloons, between our fingers, tromped the hundred bearded dandelions, bled together using crushed juices from thorned bayberries. We made a covenant of friendship, licking the pulse above our right palms, hands fisted, we spread saliva by crossing our wrists: Forever!

Here, here was my primary rite of innocence, the original trust relationship, my first love. Before this child paradise disappeared, before sexual awareness slithered come-hither into my consciousness, I had a soul-friend. And now, nearing fifty, holding this remembered reality up to the light for comparison, I am finding soul-friends again. I am healing from being born a woman, from a kind of ritual expulsion. A man stands at the door to say good-bye. His clergy collar marks fealty to God and to religious vows. Trust passes and laughs at me; I am befuddled to recognize its face. A man leans across the lunch counter. The truth of his simple statement can't be denied: *Then he doesn't know you.* Peace crooks a finger and bids me trot behind. My own three sons regard me with favor. A brother loves me. The sound of playing children soughs in my ear. My husband, a workaholic, is recovering. Laughter again is heard in my land, chortles floating upward like soap bubbles before the sunshine. I am the wife of a recovering workaholic. I have a son-in-law who calls me Mom. I remember Eden.

The ancient creation myths tell of an original androgynous human being divided into man and woman because the gods were jealous. My Scripture reveals a similar incident but sets the record straight, "Let us make man in our image," said the benevolent One-God-in-Three. "Male and female he created them, and he blessed them and named them Man when they were created" (Genesis 5:2 RSV). To some Christian theologians, Adam was not a solitary bachelor in the garden. Adam was man and woman undivided. To these scholars, after Adam was divided, there was Ish (male) and

Ishshah (female). In other words, there were the Adamses (Ish Adam and Ishshah Adam). This thinking is also part of Jewish tradition. Rashi, a famous rabbi (1040–1105), declares, "The Midrash explains that man as first created consisted of two halves, male and female, which were afterwards separated."

Through sexual union, the one made two become one flesh again; through emotional intimacy, man and woman can find psychological reunion. The Adamses communed with God. The *Living Bible* paraphrases this Scripture in a charming trimeter:

> *So God made man like his Maker.*
> *Like God did God make man;*
> *Man and maid did he make them.*

(I can hear a chant, sung by children, tongues tripping over the alliteration, "Man and maid and Maker/Maid and Maker and man.") Here is an original triad again, a sacred paradigm of all first-love relationships, unity and harmony rolling down. God at peace with Adam. Trust between Ish and Ishshah. Woman and man, co-regents in the garden. It was only after their disobedience that the Creator cried longingly, "Where are you? Adam? (Ish? Ishshah?)" Then, fallen, shaming and blaming, they abandoned co-regency; and as God had foretold, the two brought the curse down upon themselves. Hierarchical dominion was exercised only after this tragedy. The divided Adam named the woman Eve (the one who makes babies). Now Christ is the new Adam, the undivided One. In him, Ish and Ishshah are at peace. There must be a truce between the sexes if we are to model God.

So I was fortunate to have a childhood of contented first

love. I don't remember ever being abused, or coming teary-eyed and whining to my mother, insisting that she adjudicate between Allen and me. Nor did I ever run wailing to her to protect me from his aggressions. He was safe; he was just. I remember multitudinous birthday parties. Allen was a sibling among many. His brother and sisters, older and younger, ricocheted around us, teasing, interrupting, but we had no need to expand our circle of two to include them. We were complete in each other. Even then, my early intuitions forming, I knew that my friend Allen was somehow on the periphery of his family's emotional energy. His brown eyes grew watchful in the commotion, he became withdrawn. But with me he belonged, he was an insider, he had a place. We laughed together.

Our mothers, Allen's and mine, were both efficient secretaries; they contracted for homework and typed mailing labels to earn extra funds. Our mothers conferred about their business, they talked over the phone, they shared recipes and plotted mutual family events. Mothers enable their children's playful unions. They rented a two-flat, a summer cottage in Winona Lake, Indiana, a Bible Conference Center, to which we children were transported. Our fathers commuted by train on the weekends from their work in the city.

That was the summer in which innocence was lost, and I fell from triune peace. A pretender entered our Eden. An older boy, one morning when our mothers were away, took me by the hand and pulled me under the covers of the daybed. He had a new game he wanted to teach me, he said. "You can't come," I taunted my first-friend. "You can't be part of our new game." The innocuous sexual exploration became a lesson gained without much loss and kept me virginal for marriage. That day I learned never to let an older male take me by the hand into any hiding place to teach me anything. Caution. Caution.

I will never forget my first-friend taking quiet shelter in a cupboard and waiting, waiting for the game from which he had been excluded to end. He was an outsider now with me, and I had cast him out. The shame I felt was not due to entrapment but to my own treachery. Trust had been broken with me, and, overwhelmed now by knowledge, I in turn broke trust with the one I loved.

Before I started fourth grade, my parents moved to the western suburbs of Chicago. I rarely saw my friend; distance now intervened. When we were in junior high, his family moved (probably due to further maternal collusion) to our town. My girlfriends and I jostled with one another, pretending casualness; standing outside the glass of the principal's office, we caught a peek at the newcomer. Here was my first-friend, in quarter-profile, grown, olive-handsome still, his back to the hallway, tight jeans stretching as he leaned lonely over the counter, registering for classes.

Four years had passed between us. Painful self-consciousness was a dividing wall. Innocence had long been disturbed by rising sexuality, by an urgent junior-high physicality. In seventh grade, I was hopelessly in love with a rogue whose ribald jokes in art class turned my cheeks scarlet but whose startling blue/gray, cloudy eyes and hooked grin made me an emotional slave. I forgot my first love. (Is forgetfulness another form of treachery? Of course. Of course.) But now, entering this season of remembrance, he is here again, the child. Today, I measure all my soul-friends against this first: Is there innocence? Is there co-regency? Is trust present, and peace? Can we unself-consciously play? If so, then a safe and holy community is being created between us. Marriage is a sacrament that mediates Trinity, but holy friendship between men and women is also an eschatological sign of what God intends creation to be on that day when profound restoration finally comes.

Whenever I think of Trinity Sunday, I remind myself of the solace of first loves. Trinity Sunday celebrates the original first love, the unity that exists in the Divine Threesome, one of the greatest dogmas of the faith. During the first thousand years of Christianity, there was no special day set aside to observe this mystery. After the Arian heresy, in time the festival was accepted into the official calendar of the Western church and observed on the Sunday after Pentecost.

These years, I am chasing Trinity. Each Sunday, I hear the cry in my heart, "*Sursum corda!* Lift up your hearts!" I lift up my heart to the Trinity. I will learn from the One-God-in-Three that I am molded best by relationship, that I am incomplete without dialogic formation, that I can only become what God intended me to be by humbling myself to reciprocity. Each Sunday, the liturgy begins with these very words, "Blessed be God: Father, Son and Holy Spirit." Each Sunday at the communion rail, I lift my imploring hands and receive the broken bread from the warm and gentle hands of a man. But each *Trinity* Sunday, knowing now what I know about first-loves, I assess my soul. I remind myself that in Christ men and women must heal this divided Adam. We must come together in safe and holy community and model God.

Ish-Adam (I am crying as I track triads), where are you? The Pretender has played havoc with us, we are wrenched ragged, torn apart. I most earnestly forgive you and do most humbly *beg* forgiveness. In all wholeness, in all holiness, can we together find first love again? Let us restore. Let us hold reunions. In the play by Edmund Rostand, the dying and tragic lover, Cyrano de Bergerac, absolves Roxanne of neglect, "On the contrary! I had never known/Womanhood and its sweetness but for you. My mother did not love to look at me—/I never had a sister. . . . But you—because of you I have had one friend. . . ./Across my life, one whispering silken gown!"

If it is mother you seek, may I for a little while be she? If it is sister for which you are longing, may I call you brother? If it is innocence we seek, then the One-God-in-Three will make us clean again. Come (My friend! My friend!), chase Trinity with me.

TRANSFIGURATION

—◆—

Madeleine L'Engle

Sister Egg left the convent with the shopping cart. Over her simple habit she wore a heavy, hooded woolen cape. Even so, she shivered as the convent door shut behind her and she headed into the northeast wind. There was a smell of snow in the air, and while it would be pleasant to have a white Christmas, she dreaded the inevitable filthy drifts and slush that would follow a city snow. She dreaded putting on galoshes. But she would enjoy doing her share of shoveling the snow off the sidewalk.

The twenty-five-pound turkey was waiting in the pantry, but she needed to get cranberries and oranges for relish, and maybe even some olives to go with the celery sticks.

There's only one Christmas a year, and it needs to be enjoyed and celebrated. She pulled her cape more closely about her. In her mind she started counting the weeks till August. The first two weeks of August were her rest time, when she went to her brother's seaside cottage and swam in the ocean, and for her that time was always transfigured and gave her strength to come back to the Upper West Side of New York City.

"Hi, Sister Egg!" It was the small child of the Taiwanese shopkeeper from whom she always bought garlic because he had the best garlic in the city. The child rushed at her and leaped into her arms, pushing the empty market cart aside. Sister Egg caught the little boy, barely managing not to fall over backward, and gave him a big hug. "Whatcha doing?" the little boy asked.

"Christmas shopping."

"Presents?"

"No. Food. Goodies." And she reached into her pocket and drew out one of the rather crumbly cookies she kept there for emergencies such as this. The little boy stuffed the cookie into his mouth, thereby rendering himself speechless, and Sister Egg walked on. The vegetable stand she was heading toward was across Broadway, so she turned at the corner and crossed the first half of the street; then the light turned red, so she stopped at the island. In Sister Egg's neighborhood islands ran down the center of Broadway, islands that were radiant with magnolia blossoms in the spring, followed by tulips, and delicately leafing trees. By August the green was dull and drooping from the heat. In December all the branches were bare and bleak.

She stood on the island, waiting for the light to change. She, too, felt bare and bleak. She felt in need of hope, but of hope for what she was not sure. She had long since come to terms with the fact that faith is not a steady, ever-flowing stream but that it runs over rock beds, is sometimes dry, sometimes overflows to the point of drowning. Right now it was dry, dryer than the cold wind that promised snow.

"Hi, Sister Egg." She turned to see a bundle of clothes on one of the benches reveal itself to be an old woman with her small brown dog on her lap, only the dog's head showing, so wrapped were woman and dog in an old brown blanket.

"Hello, Mrs. Brown." Sister Egg tried to smile. It was Christmas Eve, and no one should spend it wrapped in an inadequate blanket, sitting on a bare island on upper Broadway. But she had learned long ago that she could not bring every waif and stray she saw out in the streets back to the convent. It was not that anybody thought it was a bad idea; it was just that the Sisters were not equipped to handle what would likely be hundreds of people hungry in body and spirit. They had taken pains to learn of every available shelter and hostel, and the hours of all the soup kitchens.

Sister Egg had tried to get this particular old woman into a home for the elderly with no success. Mrs. Brown had her share of a room in a Single Room Occupancy building. She had her dog and her independence and she was going to keep both.

From the opposite bench came a male voice, and another bundle of clothes revealed itself to be a man whose age was anybody's guess. "Sister *what?*"

"Oh—" Sister Egg looked at him, flustered.

"Sister Egg," the old woman announced triumphantly.

"Sister Egg! Whoever heard of a Sister named Egg? What are you, some kind of nut?" The scowl took over the man's body in the ancient threadbare coat as well as his face, which was partly concealed by a dark woolen cap.

Sister Egg's cheeks were pink. "My real name is Sister Frideswide. People found it hard to pronounce, so I used to say that it was pronounced 'fried,' as in fried egg. So people got to using Egg as a nickname."

"What the hell kind of a name is Frideswide?" The man's scowl seemed to take up the entire bench.

"She was an abbess in Oxford, in England, in the eighth century."

"What's an abbess?" The man sounded as though he would leap up and bite her if her answer didn't satisfy him.

"She's—she's someone who runs—runs a religious order," Sister Egg stammered.

"So what else about her?"

Did he really want to know? And how many times had the light already turned to green? And she was cold. "She was a princess, at least that's what I was told, and she ran away rather than be coerced into a marriage she didn't want."

"So she married God instead?"

"Well. Yes, I guess you could put it that way." What an odd man.

"And merry Christmas to you," he said.

She looked up just as the light changed from green to yellow to red. Wishing him merry Christmas in return was obviously not the right thing to do. She hesitated.

"And give me one reason why it should be merry. For me. For her." He jerked his chin in the direction of the old woman.

Why, indeed, should it be merry? Sister Egg wondered. There were thousands homeless and hungry in the city. Even though soup kitchens would be open for the holidays, and although volunteers would make an attempt at serving a festive meal, the atmosphere of a soup kitchen, usually in a

175

church basement, was bleak. A basement is a basement is a basement, even with banners and Christmas decorations.

"Well?" the man demanded.

"I'm not sure it's supposed to be merry," Sister Egg said. "I'm not sure when 'merry' came into it. It's a time to remember that God came to live with us."

"That was pretty stupid," the man said. "Look where it got him."

Mrs. Brown's face peered out of the old blanket. "You hadn't ought to talk like that."

A young man on a bicycle rode through the red light. He carried a large transistor radio which blared out, "Joy to the world, the Lord is come!"

"Joy, joy, joy." The man spat the words out. "What good did it do, this Lord coming? People were bad then, and they aren't any better now. Fighting. Bombing. Terrorism."

"You're upsetting Sister," Mrs. Brown said.

Sister Egg watched the light change yet again from green to yellow to red. "It's all right," she told Mrs. Brown. "Really it's all right."

"What's all right?" the man demanded.

"It's all right to say what you feel. Only—"

"Only what?"

"I don't have any answers for you."

"Thank God," the man said.

Sister Egg smiled. "Do you?"

"Hell, no. Thank *you*."

Sister Egg shivered. "I really have to make the next light."

"You're not warmly enough dressed," Mrs. Brown chided.

"Oh, I'm fine, as long as I keep moving."

The man stood up, and Mrs. Brown's little dog barked.

"Shut up, mutt. What're you doing tonight, Sister?"

If she heard the suggestiveness in his voice, Sister Egg gave no sign. "We always go to the cathedral for midnight mass. Are you coming, Mrs. Brown?"

"Sure," the old woman said. "I been coming since you first told me it was okay. Beautiful. All those candles. And the music. And people smiling and being nice."

"Yeah, and they come around with silver plates and expect you to put all your money in."

"Sister Egg puts in something for me," Mrs. Brown said. "Anyhow, you don't have to pay God."

"Yeah? And who pays for all those candles? You got to pay somebody."

The light changed to green. Sister Egg fumbled in her deep pocket. It would never do to give the man one of the crumbled cookies. Then her fingers touched something more solid, and her fingers pulled out a silver-foil-wrapped chocolate kiss. She dropped it in his lap, then started across the street, feeling herself flush as she heard him making smacking kissing noises after her.

I should have had some answers for him, she thought. I should have known what to say.

A flake of snow brushed her cheek. She hurried to her favorite vegetable store and bought cranberries and oranges and some good celery for celery sticks, and a bunch of celery that had been marked down and a bag of onions for the turkey stuffing.

"Merry Christmas, Si'r Egg." The Korean man at the cash register greeted her, and charged her half price for the oranges.

She would have to hurry. Christmas Eve Vespers and

the blessing of the crib was at five, and the chapel would be full of children from the school, and parents, too, and there would be hot, spiced cider afterward, and cookies.

It was always a special time for the children. They sat through the singing of Vespers, restless, but then there was the procession to the crèche, with the shepherds adoring, and the wise men still far off, because they couldn't arrive till Twelfth Night. And food! In half an hour the cookie plates would be empty, and the Sisters had been baking for weeks.

What did the children think? Was it all cookies and fruit cake and presents? Did they think at all about God coming to live with human beings as a human being, or was it only a baby in a manger? Did they see the shadow of the cross, and failure, thrown darkly across the golden singing of the angels?

Hearts were hard two thousand years ago. Hearts were still hard.

She started to cross Broadway again, but the light had already been green when she started so, again, she was stopped at the island.

Mrs. Brown was gone. That was all right. She would see her after the midnight mass.

But the man was there.

And she still had no words of comfort. For him. For herself.

"Take me there," the man said.

Startled, she nearly dropped the bag of onions. "Where?"

"To the church. The cathedral."

It was not far. One block south, one block east. But there was no time. "Mother Cat won't like it if I'm late," she started.

"Mother *what*?" he roared.

"Oh—Mother Catherine of Siena."

"Is there a Sister Hen and a Mother Dog? Do you all have idiot nicknames?"

"Oh, no, and we don't *call* her Mother Cat, you know, it's Mother Catherine of—"

"But she calls you Egg?"

"Sometimes it's Frideswide."

He snorted. Rose. "Let's go."

"But—"

"Here. I'll carry your bags." He took the heaviest one, which contained the cranberries and oranges.

She could leave him. She was quite capable of saying, "I'm sorry, I can't be late for Vespers." She could direct him to the cathedral, she—

"Hi, Sister Egg." It was Topaze, one of the children who was in the school. His father was in and out of jail. His mother looked as though if she spat, nails could come out of her mouth. Topaze looked like an angel. "Can I carry your bags?"

"You know I can't pay you anything, Topaze," she said. The child picked up quarters and occasionally a dollar by doing errands.

"Hey, Sister Egg, merry Christmas!" And he took the bags out of her arms, leaving her empty handed. "Where're we going?"

"To the cathedral," she said. "Mr., uh—I don't know your name."

"Joe," the man said.

"Mr. Joe wants to go to the cathedral. If you'll carry the bags to the convent and give it to one of the Sisters, you won't be late for Vespers."

"What about you?" Topaze asked.

"I guess I'll be late. Tell them not to worry about me, Topaze. I'll come as soon as I can."

"Unh unh, Sister Egg. I'm staying with you and Joe. Merry Christmas, Joe."

"Merry yourself." Once again Joe's scowl seemed larger than his body. "Let's go."

Sister Egg knew that Topaze didn't want to miss Vespers. Nevertheless she was glad to have him accompanying her, especially when they turned off brightly lit Broadway to the much darker east-bound street.

The cathedral loomed at the far end, the large and handsome lamps in front of it brightly lit. Another flake brushed Sister Egg's face, but the snow had not really begun yet; there was just an occasional flake drifting down from the low clouds.

People were already starting up the steps in small groups, to be sure of finding seats, even though they would have to wait for hours. A few greeted Sister Egg. Topaze walked on her left, holding her hand. Joe walked on her right, his threadbare coat hanging loosely. But his feet did not shuffle and his scowl was fierce.

They walked up the steps, an odd trio, Sister Egg thought, and she felt a wave of compassion flow out of her and over the man whose coat had once seen very much better days. The boy squeezed her hand.

Once they were in the vast nave of the cathedral, they stopped and looked around. The clusters of people hurrying forward to claim seats seemed small and few in that enormous space. Both sides of the nave were lined with bays, small chapels in themselves. There was a bay for St. Francis, a bay for education, a bay where a long-dead bishop was buried. Joe stopped at the bay of the Transfiguration, where there was an enormous painting that had been given the cathedral, of Jesus, James, John and Peter on the Mount of Transfiguration. Jesus' face and garments were brilliant even in the semi-darkness of the cathedral, but through and behind him was the shadow of a cross. Depending on the angle at which one looked at the picture, Jesus was transfigured with light, or his outstretched arms were on the cross. It was a stunning painting, and the bay was one of Sister Egg's favorites.

Joe put his hand against his chest, and his scowl became a grimace. "Water," he choked. "I need water."

"Topaze." Sister Egg pushed the boy in her urgency. "You know where to go. Hurry to the choir rooms and get a glass of water, quickly." Perhaps Joe needed food, too. His face was not gray. She did not think he was having a heart attack.

As soon as Topaze had put the bags of groceries down at Sister Egg's feet and vanished into the shadows, Joe braced himself against one of the stone columns of the bay, then reached out and grabbed Sister Egg's wrist. "Don't scream. Don't try to run. Give it to me."

"What?" She tried to pull away from his grasp, not understanding.

"Your money. I know you have some. You didn't spend it all on two bags of groceries."

For this she was going to be late for Christmas Eve Vespers. Even if Mother Cat—Mother Catherine of Siena—was not angry with her, the other Sisters would be. Sister Egg was always late, always stopping to speak to people.

"Come on, Egg," Joe said.

She was angry. "Couldn't you even call me a good egg?" She demanded. "Couldn't you just have asked me for it? 'Sister, I need money.' That's all you'd have needed to say."

"I don't ask for things."

"I only have a couple of dollars left. You're welcome to them." With her free hand she reached into her pocket. Pulled out a handful of crumbling cookies. "Here." Three more chocolate kisses.

"Come off it." He let her wrist go but reached for her pocket, putting his hand in and turning the pocket inside out. A small wooden cross fell to the stone floor. Some knotted woolen prayer beads. A can opener. A dog biscuit. A tiny sewing kit. "Christ, what are you, a walking dime store?"

She looked past his head to the painting of Jesus, and now all she saw was the man on the cross. The body of the dying Christ was richly muscled. It was a strong man who hung there. Joe moved toward her impatiently, and his face came between Sister Egg and Jesus, and by some trick of the dim lighting in the nave, Joe's face looked like that of the man on the cross.

"Well, there you are," she said.

He pulled two dollars and a few coins out of her turned-out pocket. "It's not enough."

"Oh yes it is," she said. "It's more than enough." She gestured toward the painting. "God cared enough to come and be one of us, and just once during his life on earth he revealed his glory. We matter to God. We matter that much."

"Don't shout," Joe growled.

"That's why it's merry Christmas." She hardly heard him. "Not that he died. But that he cared enough to be born. That's the whole point of it all. Not the Crucifixion and the Resurrection but that God cared enough to be born. That was the real sacrifice. All the power and glory of all the galaxies—" Again she waved her arm toward the painting, and now she could not see the cross, only the glory.

She stopped for breath as Topaze hurried up with a glass of water.

Joe said, "Give it to Sister Fried Egg. She needs it more than I do."

Topaze looked at them suspiciously.

"We matter that much," Sister Egg repeated wonderingly.

Joe said, "She spilled some stuff. Help her pick it up." Two dollar bills floated to the floor. Coins dropped.

Topaze squatted and picked up Sister Egg's assorted treasures, then slipped them, one by one, into her pocket.

Joe handed him the remains of the cookies. "Here, kid, these are for you. I'll keep these." His open hand held three silver-foil-wrapped chocolate kisses. Light from somewhere in the cathedral touched them so that the silver was bright.

Sister Egg found that she was holding a glass of water. When she turned to Joe, he was gone. She saw only the back of a man in a worn coat walking away.

"You all right?" Topaze asked anxiously. "You want the water?"

She took a sip. She could shout, "Thief!" and someone would stop Joe. Her wrist was sore where he had grabbed her. He was not a nice man.

She looked again at the painting. The face on the cross was Joe's. She turned so that the light shifted, and she saw the transfigured Christ.

"If we hurry," she said to Topaze, "we may miss Vespers, but we'll get there for the blessing of the crèche and the baby in the stable."

ALL SAINTS

William Griffin

The most common unit of measure with regard to saints seems to be a communion and, at least since apostolic times, there seems to have been only one such measure.

But I don't like the communion of saints.

That is to say, I don't like the "communion" of saints.

Well, I don't exactly dislike the word "communion." I know that it's derived from the Latin word for "common," which itself is made up of two words, one meaning "with," the other meaning "wall" or "fortification" or even "a walled city." I know also that the Latin word was preceded by a Greek word, *koinonia*, indicating that holy people, saintly people, once they have died, have a lot in common with each other.

But how I wish there were a better word, perhaps a more contemporary way, to describe the spiritual solidarity that binds together the faithful on earth and the saints in Heaven! The word "communion" as it appears in the Apostles' Creed is a collective noun; that is to say, a noun whose form is singular but whose meaning is plural; like the words *jury, army, police; grouse, deer, sheep; cod, trout, salmon*. These workaday words abound in the language, and indeed a language without them cannot leap and bound.

In cleverer hands, however, some collective nouns may become artifacts. A collection of bishops may be a *synod*; of cardinals, a *college*; of angels, a *choir*; of geese, a *gaggle*; of lions, a *pride*.

James Lipton, in his book *An Exaltation of Larks*, which explores the medieval practice of coining picturesque collectives, lists such well-known and well-used ones as a *school* of fish, a *bevy* of beauties, a *string* of ponies, a *covey* of partridges, a *plague* of locusts, and a *colony* of ants.

After reading Lipton's short but informative, even entertaining book, one gets the hang of creating collectives of one's own. There can be a *giggle* of girls, a *huddle* of boys, a *mausoleum* of morticians, a *Heifitz* of violins, a *Schwarzkopf* of generals, even an *Oreck* of anteaters.

When they are built on metaphors, collectives take the up escalator to new levels of meaning. I once confected the following collectives of imprisonment in the peroration to a perfectly dull speech: "In what *Alcatraz* of ignorance, in what *Sing Sing* of psychology, in what *Leavenworth* of laissez-faire . . ."

Still in search of the perfect collective for saints, I sometimes ask, Why can't there be a *bouquet* of saints, not a few of whom died in the odor of sanctity? A *sorites* of saints, linked together, arm in arm, like a chain of syllogisms? A *concelebration* of saints? A *thesaurus* of saints? An *aureole/halo/ nimbus* of saints? Since I live in New Orleans, I suppose I can even put forward something like a *superdome* of saints . . .

Who are the saints, anyway? Well, in the early days of the church, martyrs were remembered on the anniversary of their passing, their death-days becoming their birthdays in the Lord. Exceptionally slow to accept the rise of the new Christian cult, however, were the Roman Emperors. Hence, under their reign, from Nero to Diocletian, the number of martyrs increased dramatically in the first three centuries. Hence also, the number of free days in the Christian *Kalendarium* decreased just as dramatically. Finally, in the fourth century, one day in the year was set aside to commemorate all the saints, mainly the lesser ones and indeed the unknown ones who could not fit into the rest of the year; in a way, these saints could be called "the unfit."

Precisely where in the galaxy is this communion of saints? Well, since John A. T. Robinson, late Anglican theologian and Bishop of Woolwich, whose wooly thinking made C. S. Lewis refer to him as the Bishop of Woolworth, Heaven can no longer safely be called "up." If not up, then, it's certainly not down; and it's probably not east or west or any other point on the compass. Maybe Tolkien or Lewis or other creators of parallel worlds knew where it was but weren't telling. Wherever it was and indeed is, William F. Buckley, Jr., has always insisted that Heaven is a place, not a condition, and hence the word *Heaven* should be capitalized. Hence also, until the cartologists—celestial or otherwise—are able to position it with a greater degree of accuracy, I shall refer to

Heaven not only as up but also as a place with housing, or at least with accommodations. "In my father's mansion," quotes John of Jesus (14:2), "there are many rooms." But if the saints have long ago filled the calendar to overflowing, haven't they also overbooked the heavenly mansion to the point where there are cots in the lobby? Won't the Jerusalem Hilton and the King David Hotel have to be called upon for additional space? Congregating in ever-increasing circles, will not the poor saints begin to appear, inkily, lacily, like the multitudinous, and at the same time anonymous, figures in a drawing by Hans-Georg Rauch?

Assuming that the communion of saints has found (American), or have found (British), at least a bed-and-breakfast in the heavenly Jerusalem, I am forced to ask: Just what do the saints do all day long? Are they huddled like angels before the throne of God, their wings folded humbly over their heads? If they are, do you suppose some one rascal will peek out from under? There has to be some hilarity in Heaven, I should think, considering how many obstacles the various Christian theologies have strewn in the poor saints' way; there has to be some sense of having finally overcome. But how is that hilarity expressed? I mean, does everybody do the same thing? What happens to all the traits that made us sometimes irritating, sometimes interesting, on earth? Most especially I want to know, will there be humor in Heaven? Not so, thinks philosopher Mortimer Adler; certainly not among the angels, for their knowledge is infused, immediate, unencumbered; the feathery creatures, alas, would know the bloody punch lines even before they could be blabbed. But what about humankind? Can one joke and jape and caper about in Heaven? I profoundly hope so.

One school of hagiologists thinks that whatever else the

saints do up in Heaven, they'll be able to look down. "The floor of Heaven is like a window with a muslin curtain across it; we can't see in, but the saints can see out," wrote Ronald A. Knox in *The Creed in Slow Motion*, a collection of talks he gave in a British country girls school during World War II. "They see what we are doing, and are interested in what we are doing; the Epistle to the Hebrews compares them to spectators looking down on a race. If you are ever feeling rather down-hearted about your second-rate efforts to live a good Christian life," he told the girls, even as German bombs fell on their parents in London, "think of the saints in Heaven bending over the balconies in front of them and shouting out 'Stick it!' as people do when they are watching a race."

If the saints in Heaven are looking down, then the saints on earth—the people still shlepping their solitary way on the earthly pilgrimage—are looking up. As the cult of saints grew, it was only natural that the faithful, tired of petitioning a seemingly unresponsive God, pressed the saints in Heaven to do some heavy messenger work. Such practices led Reformation theologians to conclude that the faithful on earth were not only praying to the saints but also worshipping them. That the Roman Church had always distinguished three levels of worship, *latria, hyperdulia, dulia*, and that the bottommost—*dulia*, adoration at its most dilute—was reserved for the saints, didn't seem to help. The appearance remained in the eyes of Protestants that Catholics, whenever they addressed the likes of Francis of Assisi or Clare of Assisi, were praying *to* the saints, an idolatrous practice if ever there was one.

But are they really? "The consoling thing is that while Christendom is divided about the rationality, and even the lawfulness, of praying *to* the saints," wrote C. S. Lewis in

Letters to Malcolm, Chiefly on Prayer, "we are all agreed about praying *with* them. 'With angels and archangels and all the company of Heaven . . .' One always accepted this *with* theoretically. But it is quite different when one brings it into consciousness at an appropriate moment and wills the association of one's own little twitter with the voices of the great saints and (we hope) of our own dear dead. They may drown some of its uglier qualities and set off any tiny value it has."

"In this, as in all other feasts of the saints," wrote Catholic priest Alban Butler in the middle of the eighteenth century when he compiled a multivolume work entitled *The Lives of the Fathers, Martyrs and Other Principal Saints,* "God is our only object of supreme worship, and the whole of that lesser and different veneration which is paid to them is directed to give sovereign honor to Him alone, whose gifts their graces are; and our prayers to them are only petitions to holy fellow-creatures for the assistance of their prayers to God for us. When, therefore, we honor the saints, in them and through them we honor God, and Christ, true God and true man, the redeemer and savior of mankind, the king of all the saints, the source of their holiness and glory."

Saints in Heaven have their earthly uses. They have been construed as patrons of everything from midwifery to fishmongery and are implored accordingly; and they have been proposed, usually by the clergy, as models of people who've made it. Trouble is that most of what we know about the saints has been transmitted to us in written form. Many of the earliest accounts are filled with midrashic mush. And in later accounts there is the tendency—lamentable in any age— to flash forward: that is to say, to describe earlier events in a person's life in the light of his or her saintly death. That way the biographer creates a sort of romantic, violin-accompanied uni-time, and concludes that if the life ended well, then all of its components were equally good. That way also lies mush, a sort of no-fault history, no-warts hagiography, better than Sominex in producing a drowse.

As for the communion of saints on earth, when I try to envision them, I seem to see a crowd, not a polite crowd such as one might find in a Renaissance painting, Brueghel excluded, but a live crowd, an impatient crowd, a surging crowd, too many to fit comfortably in one place, 250 people in a container barely big enough for 100. For the reekers and roilers, it's either too hot (the air conditioning isn't working), or it's too cold (the air conditioning is working).

I can limn the image even further. Gentlemen listening to Torah tapes. Gentlewomen saying rosaries. Some leafing their Scriptures; other loafing through their devotionals. I wouldn't be surprised if there are Muslims perusing the Koran. There are the well-dressed and the ill-dressed, the sighted and the unsighted, those who can hear and those who have hearing aids. And there's probably someone squawking about a systemic disease, working her way through the crowd and collecting coins in a can to fight it.

That, I think, is my rather large-scale image, my raggedy canvas, of the communion of saints on earth—*a New York City subway car during rush hour*—and what better image can there be than that, a graffiti-covered, ten-car train, people of all sorts stuffed like clothespins onto a plastic-covered line, careening through the blistering heat or numbing cold toward—"A little traveling music, Sammy!" as Jackie Gleason used to say—toward the communion of saints in Heaven?

ALL SOULS

~

Shirley Nelson

I am certain Eileen Calihan must have told me about All Souls' Day, since she had a lot to say about purgatory and prayer for the dead. It was Eileen who instructed me in all the Roman mysteries—the essential dogma, the sacraments, the various and most interesting kinds of sin, the movable and unmovable days of fast and feast. We were fourteen at the time, whiling away a rainy week at Girl Scout camp in the woods of Massachusetts.

I suppose I started the thing. I had just begun to read the Bible and had brought a tiny New Testament to camp, where I opened it each morning in my bunk, hoping a bit that my friends would notice and hoping very much they would not.

Eileen was the single one of my nine tent-mates curious enough to ask about the little book, and in answer I favored her with my secret. My secret was recent conversion—not to Catholicism, obviously, but to the innermost heart of Protestantism. I had been saved, by grace, by unearned mercy, by Christ's eternally effective substitutionary atonement, from all my sins (past, present, and future), from the wrath of God, from the threat of hell, from the necessity of purgatory (as I soon argued to Eileen), and I had become, by personal choice, all by myself, without the faintest shadow of an institution rising behind me, without benefit of baptism, ordination, or canonization, a Christian, a priest, and a saint.

Eileen, horrified, proceeded to set me straight, with both shadow and substance rising behind her, not only the authority of the ancient Mother Church, but a goodly portion of the town we lived in. I had learned early in school, when matters of heritage came up, not to broadcast my alleged lineage to Peregrine White, the alleged first baby born on the Mayflower. I had found it much more acceptable to boast about the one-quarter of my blood that was allegedly Irish, my maternal grandmother's maiden name being Collins. There were three churches in our town, Congregational, Baptist, and Roman Catholic. The Roman Catholic, St. Mary's, was by far the largest, its communicants the Italian and Irish population that had been drawn over the generations to the thriving shoe industry along the railroad tracks.

I myself had been raised virtually churchless. My siblings and I attended the Congregational church when we felt like it, more for social reasons than piety or politics. Within the stark simplicity of its sanctuary, outward symbols of faith were not accentuated. No creed was required for membership. Other than Christmas and Easter, no holy days were celebrated. Our two sacraments, baptism and communion, carried no momentous significance. Nobody in town with an ounce of self-promotion belonged to the Baptist church, but at least it housed the intrigue of immersion. Going all the way under with your clothes on made a statement. At the Congregational church baptism was about as exciting as dipping your big toe into the town lake on a hot July day. As for communion, at the Catholic church you not only received it every Sunday, the process itself took a magical turn that shot it out of the ordinary. At the Congregational church, our monthly communion service wore the air of a tiresome tea, made bearable only by the hope and dread that somebody might upend a tray of those dainty little glasses as they were carried from pew to pew. While deacons lumbered up and down the aisles, and stomachs growled and children fussed, across the street the Catholics efficiently fed their 5,000 (or so it seemed) with the body of Christ and sent them home.

My conversion had no connection to the church. It resulted from a one-on-one conversation with a young woman I admired. She herself had been converted while reading a novel by Grace Livingston Hill and had subsequently been schooled in the premillennial dispensational view of Scripture, which is to say, very precisely, American Protestant Fundamentalism. My "decision for Christ," more cerebral than emotional, seemed the right and sensible thing to do. Any doubts that followed related only to the rash promise to pray and read the Bible daily, a covenant I made to gain the approval of my mentor, who also commissioned me to confess my new-found faith to my friends as soon as "the Spirit led."

Eileen, as it turned out, was the first to hear. Our peculiarity bonded us instantly. We knew of no one else in our age group who had ever admitted openly to being "religious." If we differed on the finer points, we recognized the superiority of our common impulse. Eileen judged my experience to be satisfactory as far as it went, and I approved the sincerity of her faith, though I had no use for the additives she proposed. The veneration of Mary, the graven images of saints, the sweet logic of doing penance all seemed gratuitous to me, and most particularly the need for a purgatorial adjustment of the balances after death. I had no means for articulating the sweet absurdity of unconditional atonement; I just liked it a whole lot better.

I should explain that this private ecumenical conference met in the pre-Vatican II year of 1940. Recently, in the course of casual research, I turned up a treatise on purgatory written in that same year. Purgatory is something like an exile, reads this document, temporary (if we think in terms of time), a place (if we think in terms of space) full of sorrow and pain, where the baptized soul "is detained for spiritual debts it failed to meet on earth." In the course of intense suffering the soul is purified, made perfect, in preparation for entering the presence of God. Suffering is the key to everything, the Catholic reader is reminded. To avoid a stretch in purgatory one must welcome wholeheartedly all the hardships of life on earth in a spirit of true penitence.

That happens to be exactly what Eileen told me, and if I viewed with skepticism the everlasting value of such Brownie points, I could hardly question Eileen's own knowledge of suffering. She had lost her father the year before our Scout camp encounter. She was an only child, adored and a little spoiled—the first among our friends to have a real birthday party, the first to get a permanent wave—and her dad, handsome and witty, had been a favorite son of the town and the parish. I realize now how young he was, surely no more than his late thirties, when he died suddenly of an acute attack of appendicitis.

It was the first death for a lot of us in our class, a first death that caught our full empathy. We could feel the life-altering quality of it. Nothing, nothing ever the same again. Eileen remained out of school for several weeks, praying every day in church, we were told, and when she returned we flocked around her and stared, awed, smiling shyly, touching her hand, peering into her face to see if she had changed. She was quiet and pale, and it seemed to me she had grown substantially taller.

Others in our class had been suffering for as long as we had known them, but we never thought of them in that manner. We ignored their pain, if we—or they—even recognized it as pain: Reva Anderson, whose father was an alcoholic and either neglected or beat her; Arty Mason, deformed at birth, lame, asthmatic, unable to speak above a whisper or run on the playground; Charlie Hanover, who had lost both parents at an early age, one to suicide and one to mental illness, and was being raised by an aunt who worked him so hard on her farm he came to school in a stupor. Then there were the "State Children" among us, the wards, always unpopular, flunking everything and misbehaving at every opportunity. We had grown accustomed to all of these. They dragged their troubles to school each day like a pile of old books, their vacuums, their weariness, their self-hatred, their loneliness, and their phlegm. Eileen Calihan's pain was fresh and brilliant, a piercing surprise, an icicle right to the heart. Life could betray even the lucky.

She and I were not close friends at the time of her sorrow. Later, when we were religious confidants, she explained what had complicated her grief: the state of her father's soul. He had grown up a Catholic, but not as a true believer. Her beloved dad was in purgatory and nothing—not the daily candles and prayers, not the elaborate (as it seemed to me) network of special masses and offerings and sacrifices—relieved her anxiety. That took a private miracle. One day, praying alone in the church after school, she asked for a sign that her father was safely among the blest, and as she opened her eyes she saw his face exactly in the center of the stained glass rose window above the altar, smiling at her and winking.

I remember accepting this story without criticism. Whatever had happened and whatever it meant, Eileen's agony had been lifted. Wherever her dad happened to be, he was apparently all right, able to tease and smile.

I was not a complete stranger to death myself. By now all my grandparents had grown ill and died. But though I missed their presence, their absence had no jarring effect on my daily life, and I can't say I actually mourned for them. More than anything in my carefree childhood, it was the annual Memorial Day parade that awakened in my heart the notes of a song I recognized as eons old and forever new, the terrible sorrow of our human disjointedness, the inevitability of our final goodbyes.

I was very young when this started, a Brownie, marching in our wavering out-of-step lines the whole three miles behind the Girl Scout drum-and-bugle corps, the Boy Scout floats and flags, the American Legion brass band, the veterans of World War I in wrinkled uniforms, the police force, the various women's auxiliaries, all led by a black convertible bearing a gray-headed vestige of the Spanish-

American fiasco. For the last quarter mile, as we approached the Protestant cemetery, we walked in a hush, with applauding spectators left behind and the bands silent, save for one drum touched gently with the stick for each right foot step. Then even that ceased as we turned off the hot tarred road and entered the leafy lane above the lake. There among the hundreds of white grave markers we honored the dead of our wars.

As a Brownie I raced among the stones during the lengthy ceremonies, and as a Girl Scout I giggled with my friends and wondered if Bobby Bernardi was looking at me. But these were merely postures, hedges against the omens of destiny. Though as yet my family owned no plots in the cemetery, by the time I was out of high school there would be one marker, a memorial to my brother, whose remains would lie at the bottom of the Adriatic Sea. Before I was married there would be a second, the younger sister who would die in a bike accident at age twenty-one, her lovely face ruined by failed surgery and the clumsy administrations of the mortuary beautician. Years later my parents would join these two, their eldest and youngest children. Of course I knew none of this in the slightest detail. Nevertheless, the future reverberated unmistakably across the lake in the six gun salute and the bugled taps, and I was always enormously relieved when we lined up to march away.

I'm ashamed to say that I don't remember the location of the Catholic cemetery. For some reason the ceremonies were briefer there, perhaps because the Catholics had other memorial days in their year. In our town, St. Mary's kids donned their Hallowe'en masks surrounded by a saintly cloud of witnesses and dreamed of their next piece of candy with the Dies Irae of the mass for the dead in their ears: "O Day of wrath and doom impending . . . , Heaven and earth in ashes ending."

There have been many days for publicly remembering the dead in the divisions of the Roman Church over the centuries. When the list of saints and martyrs deserving honor far exceeded the days of the year, one day was set aside to celebrate the heroism of them all. And when, as the church grew larger and the world smaller, and those ordinary Christians in purgatory who had died with venial sins unremitted reckoned into astronomics, one day was set aside to pray for all of them as well. The various dates of these occasions were finally designated by Rome as the first and second days of November, All Saints and All Souls back to back, the "communion of all the faithful."

I don't know how elaborate All Souls' Day rituals were at St. Mary's when we were growing up. Universally the service was solemn, the liturgical color black, the masses Requiem. A delightful body of folklore has grown up around the day, more festive than sorrowful—long processions to cemeteries, bells tolling, the blessing and decoration of graves, hundreds of candles left flickering through the night. Like many church customs, All Saints' and All Souls' Days carry the aura of pre-Christian rites. November 1 and 2 mark the end of the harvest and the onset of the gray winter months, the demise of nature, the appeasement and entertainment of the wandering dead lost in the chronology of seasons. If they are wandering, restless, surely they must be hungry. Feed them. Leave bread and beans where poor spirits might find them—or where poor bodies certainly will. Soul food, soul bread, soul cake.

I love an old story out of rural Poland. At midnight on

All Souls' Day a bright light suddenly glows in the parish church, departed souls still in purgatory gathering at the altar where they once received the Blessed Sacrament. Throughout the next day, doors and windows in the homes round about are left open or unlocked as a sign of welcome to those who once occupied these houses. And in parts of Austria, the story goes, children are instructed to pray out loud as they take short cuts through the church grounds on All Souls' Day— not to protect themselves so much as to assure the suffering ones who hover there that they are not forgotten.

Prayer for the dead is not a traditional Protestant practice, since the basis for it in Scripture is considered questionable. But apparently some first-century Christians chose to be baptized in the name of the dead (1 Corinthians 15:29), and prayer for the dead was not unknown in the Jewish faith (2 Maccabees 12:43). Theology and Scripture aside, I wonder if the Catholic Church has not simply been more honest about our human tendencies and needs. All Souls' Day is another way to make bearable what cannot be borne. Ernest Becker, in *The Denial of Death*, claims that all our psychic energies, our systems of thought, our loves, our heroes, our wars, our rituals and beliefs are simply part of a superstructure of insistence that our lives must never end.

I grew up in a family not only Protestant but stoic. We were embarrassed by fuss, by outward demonstration. Things that mattered in life were inherently private, to the point of being tacit, simply understood. Our weeping at funerals was inward, our screams of rage echoed where only we could hear them. I remember my mother saying shortly after the death of my sister, "I'm just thankful nobody can see my insides." It was the only time I ever heard her make a remark that in her own judgment might come close to self-pity. It startled me. Yet no answer was required or appropriate. For I did see her insides and she knew it. That war zone was part of my daily scenery.

In my family you took it on the chin, kept your mouth shut and went on with life. I don't defend that strategy (and it was a strategy); I simply recognize it as how we were. We'd have felt silly lighting candles. A candle was only a candle, and the person it represented—ah, so alive, so pulsating and real, so bone of our bone, so integrated in every breath we took, registering in our voices, seeing through our eyes. A candle would seem like a mockery, as would a face in a stained glass window.

But I don't kid myself. I insist on concreteness as much as anyone else. Soul food. Metaphor. An abstract embodied in a tangible, creating a new whole, a new "thing." All the solemn processions I have not followed in the street, the wreaths I have not laid, the bugles I have not blown have found their way onto the page, my dead commemorating themselves, you might say (though they'd be embarrassed at the thought) in the created life of narrative. Lighting a candle is one way, poetry is another, and we each do what we find natural and true, children praying out loud as we walk through the cemetery, so those who have gone before will know they are not forgotten.

The concept of purgatory, I am told, has softened in the Western church since 1940. "Modern interpretations see purgation in terms of maturation more than in terms of paying a debt," reads the 1988 edition of *The New Dictionary of Theology*. The 1940 treatise explained that purgatory was based on the premise of the "infinite sanctity of God, who cannot suffer in His elect the least blemish." Eileen Calihan and I might have argued about the efficacy of Christ's work on the cross, but I think we would both, at age fourteen, have liked the reading of the word "perfection" as "maturity," as adult completeness, rather than the absence of blemish.

For us both that would have meant a new conditioning, for Eileen no longer the need for the visual proof of her father's face, and for me a loosening of the armor, an opening of the book in my heart. I like to think that for both of us it might have meant the ability to hold in suspension what we cannot know as fact. The Biblical basis for purgatory is "problematic," says *The New Dictionary of Theology*. Indeed, and isn't it all? We know only in part, says Paul, like dim reflections in a mirror. He goes on to say that we are of all people "most miserable, if in this life only we have hope in Christ." Yet he calls it a *hope*, and in God's wisdom that is what it remains, however triumphant and necessary. Maybe learning to separate the freedom to hope from the compulsion to know is part of growing up.

But growth comes in irregular spurts. Our joints ache. Our hormones play tricks. In our imperfection (our immaturity) we reach for candles and for words. So in this faulty manner I memorialize my dead, and Eileen Calihan's dead, the brief purgatories of our families and friends, and the eternal hope of us all.

CHRIST THE KING

Stephen R. Lawhead

A young man is sleeping in a hut by a lake. It is near dawn. As the sky brightens in the east, a group of armed men appear. They enter the hut, seize the young man and bind his wrists with leather cords. The men carry their prisoner to a waiting boat, and the boat is pushed out into the lake. They then row the boat to an island in the center of the lake where other men are waiting.

The prisoner is brought before these men and made to kneel before them. No one speaks. They watch and wait, their faces impassive.

The sky grows gradually lighter. As the sun breaks above the horizon, the foremost man steps over the prisoner and withdraws his hand from beneath his cloak. He is holding a knife, and as the first rays of the new sun strike the youth huddled at his feet, the man raises the knife and swiftly plunges the blade into the young man's neck.

The youth makes no attempt to escape; he does not struggle or resist. He slumps silently to the ground as his lifeblood gushes forth into a bowl that is quickly set aside.

Satisfied, the murderers smile as the young man dies. And when he has breathed his last, they set upon the corpse with sharp knives, hacking strips of flesh from the body. The flesh is eaten and the bowl of blood passed hand to hand. Each man drinks, spilling a few drops upon the ground before raising the bowl to his lips. Lastly, the still-warm heart is carved from the victim's chest. This grisly treasure is presented to one of their number—another young man who has been standing by, witnessing this gruesome ritual. The youth receives the heart, slices a small piece, and eats it.

A brutal scene, I know, but not entirely fiction. The scene I have described is historical. The shocking event was enacted countless times through the earliest ages of human civilization in all corners of the world. Virtually every culture had a similar, if not identical, ritual.

The young man sacrificed was not a criminal or a slave. He was not a victim plucked from his bed by enemy raiders or a prisoner of war. He was, in fact, the most exalted member of the tribe. He was the king. And the youth who ate the king's heart became the new king who would himself be sacrificed when his reign was finished.

The king's death was necessary if the tribe was to endure and succeed in the coming year. For the king's blood poured out upon the ground ensured a bountiful harvest; his flesh, consumed by his kinsmen, guaranteed life and fertility, the increase of the tribe. The sacrifice of the king was not an act of desperation, or the final resort of a frightened, ignorant people. It was the culmination of the king's mystical career and, as such, the king suffered it gladly.

Kingship is something I have been interested in for some time. In my research into the tales of King Arthur and Merlin, I began to peel away the centuries-old veneer to discover a much older conception of sovereignty. Beneath the accumulated layers of pomp and circumstance, there stands another image—ancient as it is compelling.

The more I chipped away at the subject—wondering about the fifth-century world of Arthur and Merlin, writing their stories, following the slender and elusive narrative threads—the more I began to see that old, old picture, the universal portrait of the king. As I encountered, imaginatively, the world of Arthur and Merlin, I glimpsed the essence of the older form of kingship. And I realized that I had stumbled upon the central theme of the Gospel message itself, revealed in the ancient portrait of the king.

This primitive portrait is far removed from our modern ideas of who a king is and what he does. Like most people, I suppose the word *king* always conjured up an image of a bearded and bulgy Henry VIII in his silken hose, or a lion-hearted Richard leading a crusade, or a merry old King Cole, calling for his pipe and bowl. Whenever anyone said the word *king*, I thought of a medieval monarch sitting on a silver throne in a high castle, with his lords and ladies in attendance, and hot and cold running servants at his beck and bidding.

Yet, there was a time when the man who wore the title of king was both leader and servant, when the words *king* and *sacrifice* were synonymous. In that far-off time, no one would have had to explain the bizarre early morning ritual of the king's death. Every man, woman, and child of the tribe would have known exactly what it meant, for each of their lives was tightly entwined with the life of the king, as his life was bound to theirs. The king *was* the life of his people; he was the incarnate spirit of the tribe.

But somewhere, in dim ages past, the concept of kingship changed. Gradually, the emphasis shifted away from the king's spiritual role and centered on his temporal role. Kings became rulers, authority figures, demigods. They were no longer sacrificed but were sacrificed to. They ruled their people and presided over the fortunes of the tribe, directing the warriors in battle, delivering law from the judgment seat, collecting and distributing the wealth of the tribe.

And this is our general picture of kings today: imposing figures of regal bearing, surrounded by as much royal glitter and glamor as imagination will allow, holding court in a moat-surrounded palace, wearing a crown of gold and robes of scarlet trimmed in ermine, basking in the adulation of their low-born minions.

Today, a king is a character in a fairytale or a figure out of history. In the age of the microchip and the space shuttle, kings have about as much usefulness as signet rings and sealing wax; they are as relevant to the world of nuclear superpowers as knights in shining armor. Indeed, in the few Western countries where a sham monarchy still persists, it does so as a quaint reminder of a storybook past. Kings are living relics, animate history, real-life Disney characters kept on the public payroll to boost the tourist trade.

Devalued as it is, though, the word "king" retains a certain currency for the church. Christians enlist a number of royal epithets to describe something of the divine authority that Christ holds: King of kings, King of Israel, High King of Heaven, the Great King, King of the Ages, Priest King, and Ruler of the Kingdom of God. We call Jesus king; we call him Lord.

To be sure, the lordship of Christ is something the Bible is most adamant about. All through the pages of the testaments old and new, several Greek and Hebrew words are translated into the simple English word *lord*—a figure of supreme power and authority, one whose word is law and whose every command must be obeyed. "Lord," after all, is how one addresses a king, acknowledging not only his superiority, but also his leadership.

But I cannot help wondering how such an important word can have any real meaning to us—especially if it is only ever used to describe a fairytale figure. Americans are particularly out of their depth when praying to, singing about, and worshipping a king, a lord. Kings and kingdoms, after all, were precisely what America was formed to escape. We are an immigrant nation made up of various huddled masses who yearned to breathe freedom's fresh air, not the stale Old World fug of despotic monarchs and onerous royalty.

So here we all are, egalitarians to the last, with a fairly large gap in our collective consciousness where Christ is concerned. Lacking any fundamental understanding of kings, we therefore possess no genuine understanding of what the kingship of Christ means. We sing of Christ the King upon his heavenly throne, and we proclaim the Lordship of Christ. And though our hearts may be in the right place, we are saddled with Old King Cole and his merry old soul, rotund

Henry VIII, and the Grimm monarchs of "once upon a time" and "happily ever after."

Perhaps we can be forgiven our lapse. There is a time-honored tradition of misunderstanding the precise nature of divine kingship, beginning with the early Jews.

The whole point of a Jewish nation was to demonstrate to the world a unique new spiritual and political entity: a nation holding God as its king, a people obedient to no earthly sovereign, wholly devoted to God the Creator as Lord. And it might have worked. But Israel, being Israel, was never really keen on the idea.

From the beginning there were problems with the scheme, and these problems reached a head in the time of Samuel, around 1100 BC. Ever fearful and insecure, little Israel looked around and saw itself surrounded by the military might of its more powerful neighbors. And the people began to question the wisdom of having an invisible spirit for a king—especially when all the other nations in the neighborhood had really flash kings who paraded in chariots and wielded sharp swords. Next to these corporeal superpowers, the ethereal monarchy of God appeared a pretty tenuous and transparent affair.

So the elders of Israel plucked up their courage and confronted the aged judge Samuel, demanding that he establish an earthly king to lead them—especially in battle, which was the primary chore of a king in those days. Samuel, displeased with this development, nevertheless took the request under advisement and prayed about it. God answered him, saying, "It is not you they have rejected, it's me they no longer want as their king. But that's nothing new, they've been rejecting me since the day I rescued them from Egypt! Very well, if that's the way they want it, warn them about all the grief an earthly king will bring them."

Samuel, faithful servant, returned to the people with a grim but realistic picture of what establishing an earthly monarchy would mean. In Samuel's view, it boiled down to virtual slavery for the nation forced to support a military dictatorship. But Samuel's words fell on deaf ears; the people had their minds made up. They wanted a mortal king to gawk at, and only a mortal king would do. "All right!" replied God, when Samuel reported the people's reaction, "I will give them a king."

God acquiesced to his stubborn children and allowed them a king. Of course, Israel chose a military ruler—someone to ride out before the troops waving a spear, someone to lead the charge in battle. In fact, they chose a king exactly like the other kings in the area, a pompous man to parade around in a chariot and make them look like big news in the eyes of the world. God, however, clearly had something different in mind. Nevertheless, God gave them the king they asked for and settled back to wait.

A thousand years pass; the fortunes of Israel rise and fall, mostly fall. And the nation of Israel is once again yearning for a king: a king of military might and political power, a sword-wielding deliverer who will restore the much-faded glory of the past and exact revenge on the nation's enemies. Once again, God hears the prayer of his stiff-necked people, and he gives them a king. But this time he gives them the king he has prepared for them from the beginning. This king, however, is of the older, more primitive variety. Not the man with the swagger and the sword, but the youth who goes silently to his death, willingly laying down his life for his people.

In the fullness of time, God gave to Israel, and to the world, the king who is the sacrifice, whose body and blood is food and drink to his people, and whose death guarantees new life. To a world bedazzled by kings of vast and fearful consequence, God gave the king obedient to the death. In the fullness of time, God gave the world its only True King. He gave himself. This is the underlying meaning of kingship, and it is the kingship of Jesus, how it is and was always meant to be. And this is why, two thousand years later, we still call him "Lord."

ABOUT THE

AUTHORS

Harold Fickett is executive director of the Milton Center, an institute for Christian writers at Kansas Newman Center in Wichita. His fiction includes *Mrs. Sunday's Problem and Other Stories* and *Holy Fool*. He also serves as coeditor of *Image: A Journal of Religion and the Arts* and has written the critical biography *Flannery O'Connor: Images of Grace*.

Emilie Griffin, a writer on conversion and prayer, sometime advertising copywriter and theology student, lives with her husband, William, in New Orleans. She is author of *Turning: Reflections on the Experience of Conversion; Clinging: The Experience of Prayer;* and *Chasing the Kingdom: A Parable of Faith.* She has written and coproduced a twelve-part television series on the Bible, *Understanding God's Word.*

211

William Griffin, an editor at Macmillan Publishing Company and Harcourt Brace Jovanovich for twenty years, now resides in New Orleans with his wife, Emilie. He is the religious books editor for *Publishers Weekly* and the author of *Clive Staples Lewis: A Dramatic Life* and *The Fleetwood Correspondence: An Epistolary Novel*.

Alice Slaikeu Lawhead is the author of *The Christmas Survival Book* and other nonfiction works. She is currently writing murder mysteries from her home in Oxford, England.

Stephen R. Lawhead is a novelist from the American Midwest who is living and working in Oxford, England, with his wife, Alice, and two sons. His recent works of fiction include *The Pendragon Cycle* and *The Song of Albion*; both are trilogies.

John Leax is professor of English and poet in residence at Houghton College, where he has taught since 1968. His most recent books are *Nightwatch*, a novel; *Country Labors*, a collection of poems; and *Standing Ground*, a more detailed account of the events recorded in his essay in this book, "Lent."

Madeleine L'Engle was born in New York City, lives there, raised her children there, writes there, walks her dog there. Her newest books, *Certain Women* and *A Rock that Is Higher*, will be published in the fall of 1992.

Karen Burton Mains works in several media of communication. With her husband, David, she cohosts the daily national radio program *The Chapel of the Air*. She travels widely as a lecturer and has written such books as *Open Heart, Open Home; Karen, Karen; The Fragile Curtain;* and *Child Sexual Abuse: A Hope for Healing*.

About the Authors

Calvin Miller, pastor of Westside Church in Omaha, Nebraska, for twenty-five years, has recently been called to be a professor at Southwest Baptist Seminary in Fort Worth, Texas. He has written thirty books, recent ones being *Spirit, Word and Story* and the trilogy *A Requiem for Love*.

Shirley Nelson has published a novel, *The Last Year of the War*, and a narrative history, *Fair, Clear and Terrible: The Story of Shiloh, Maine*. She lives in Albany, New York, and occasionally teaches creative writing.

Virginia Stem Owens now spends the last half of the season after Pentecost through the season of Easter in Kansas, where she and her husband both teach English. She is currently director of the Milton Center, an institute for Christian writers at Kansas Newman Center in Wichita. The first and fresher half of the season after Pentecost she spends musing at her home in Texas.

Eugene H. Peterson, a pastor for thirty-four years, has recently accepted an appointment as professor of spiritual theology at Regent College, Vancouver, B.C. He and his wife, Janice, spend several months of the year in the Rocky Mountains of northwest Montana, writing and hiking. His most recent books are *Answering God* and *Under the Unpredictable Plant*.

Luci Shaw is writer in residence at Regent College, Vancouver. Her books include *Polishing the Petroskey Stone* (poems), *God in the Dark* (her journal on bereavement), *Life-Path* (a journaling workbook), and *Horizons: Exploring Creation* (poems and essays), illustrated by Timothy Botts. She lives in California with her husband, John Hoyte.

213

Robert Siegel's most recent book of poems is *In a Pig's Eye.* His poems have won *Poetry*'s Glatstein Prize and fellowships from Bread Loaf, the Ingram Merrill Foundation, and the National Endowment for the Arts. He is the author of several books of fiction, including *Whalesong* and *White Whale.* He has taught at Dartmouth, Princeton, and Wheaton, and is currently professor of English at the University of Wisconsin.

Walter Wangerin, Jr., occupies the Jochum Chair at Valparaiso University in Indiana. The position is modeled as writer-in-residence, allowing him lecturing privileges in every department and college of the university. He recently published *Elizabeth and the Water Troll, Reliving the Passion,* and *Mourning Into Dancing.*

Gregory Wolfe is a writer, teacher, editor, and critic. He is founder and coeditor of *Image: A Journal of the Arts and Religion.* He was educated at Hillsdale College and Oxford University. His essays and reviews have appeared in such journals as *First Things, National Review, Books and Religion,* and *New Oxford Review.* He is currently writing a critical biography of British journalist and Christian apologist Malcolm Muggeridge. He lives with his wife and three children in the Shenandoah Valley of Virginia.

Philip Yancey, former editor of *Campus Life*, now writes regularly for *Christianity Today* as editor-at-large. His ten books include *Where Is God When It Hurts?, Fearfully and Wonderfully Made, Disappointment with God,* and *I Was Just Wondering.*